Praise for Marianne Moore's

Observations

"How wonderful to have *Observations* as it was when it first appeared. Or almost. This is Moore's slightly revised 1925 version of the 1924 first edition, as strange and new and enchanting as we remember it. One's long-ago favorites are here: 'Poetry' (I too, dislike it), 'Sea Unicorns and Land Unicorns,' 'Marriage,' and above all, 'An Octopus,' one of the truly great poems of the twentieth century. In it she quotes the lines ' "complexities which still will be complexities / as long as the world lasts," ' which could be a motto for Moore's magnificent bricolage."   —John Ashbery

"If *Observations* appeared today, readers would think it the most original and game-changing poetry of this new century. One would say that Moore had transcended all the experiments of modernism to find a completely unique synthesis of the objective and the subjective— unimaginably supple verse imprinted by the science of our moment, in which what it is to be virtual, material, experienced, repurposed, could all be integrated into a poetry where a singular voice both has and does not have a place. The hypertrophic use of quotation moves the speaker's position from lyric to dramatic to epigrammatic to didactic and back in the space of a single sentence. The astonishing math of her syllabics slices and builds new realities like a 3-D printer or the marvelous precisions of astrophysics. She penetrates deep space even within resistant fractal surfaces. This brilliant slender book makes Marianne Moore feel like our future. She is."   —Jorie Graham

"I have always been awed by the glittering intelligence, immense ambition, precision, formal confidence, wit, and authentic idiosyncratic imagination of Moore's earlier poems. Reading them, I feel I am in the presence of that rare thing, a truly extraordinary poetic mind. If, instead of reading this book yet again with the greatest pleasure and admiration, I were picking it up for the first time, I would feel immediately sure

I was in the presence of an important new voice in American poetry. These poems have always seemed totally contemporary to me, and they are some of the finest ever written in the American language."

—Matthew Zapruder

"Marianne Moore's *Observations* are personal and historical, and always intensely modern. Clearly a figurehead, she's armed with a quiver of wit and perfect aim. This poet bends the natural and man-made until each turn conveys a physical intellect and a music distinctly hers. Throughout this collection, Moore's unique signature becomes a capsule of tonal time and playful contemplation through compelling imagery. This reissue of *Observations* realigns and claims Moore's place within the modernist tradition as she continues to speak to us."   —Yusef Komunyakaa

"Far from being an obscure or difficult poet, Marianne Moore is one of the most lucid poets America has ever produced. The poems in *Observations* compose a collected—and collective—inquiry into what is valuable and why, combining two kinds of 'observation': that of the natural scientist, whose whole occupation is engaged in unruffled looking; and that of the essayist, who arranges social experience into sentences that surprise us with the force of objects. In Moore's case, beautiful objects. But these poems aren't just ornaments: they are radical, like her witty poem about socialist carrots: 'wedge-shaped engine with the / secret of expansion.' I am grateful for this reissue, which restores poems all but lost to us. It is really the best of Moore in one portable volume—a poetry not of the past, it seems to me, but of the future."   —Ange Mlinko

"The sensation of reading Marianne Moore is like none other. She is the most natural, the most exotic, the most concentrated, the most circumspect, the most weirdly precise, the most beguiling poet of the twentieth century. Like explosive sunbursts, her poems sparkle with irrepressible feeling—joy, grief, desperation, triumph—and ask, What is virtue? What is vice? What is ugliness? What is a hero? What is love? She is my favorite American anti-poet."   —Henri Cole

Observations

EDITED AND WITH

AN INTRODUCTION BY

LINDA LEAVELL

FARRAR, STRAUS AND GIROUX

NEW YORK

Observations

MARIANNE
MOORE

Farrar, Straus and Giroux
18 West 18th Street, New York 10011

Library of Congress Cataloging-in-Publication Data
Names: Moore, Marianne, 1887–1972. | Leavell, Linda, 1954–
Title: Observations : poems / Marianne Moore ; introduction by Linda Leavell.
Description: New York : Farrar, Straus and Giroux, 2016. | Includes index.
Identifiers: LCCN 2015035419 | ISBN 9780374226862 (paperback) |
    ISBN 9780374713614 (e-book)
Subjects: | BISAC: POETRY / American / General.
Classification: LCC PS3525.O5616 O3 2016 | DDC 811/.52—dc23
LC record available at http://lccn.loc.gov/2015035419

Designed by Jonathan D. Lippincott

Our books may be purchased in bulk for promotional, educational,
or business use. Please contact your local bookseller or the Macmillan Corporate
and Premium Sales Department at 1-800-221-7945, extension 5442, or by e-mail
at MacmillanSpecialMarkets@macmillan.com.

www.fsgbooks.com
www.twitter.com/fsgbooks • www.facebook.com/fsgbooks

1 3 5 7 9 10 8 6 4 2

CONTENTS

INTRODUCTION BY LINDA LEAVELL

It took some arm-twisting to get Marianne Moore to publish *Observations*, the book that in 1924 established her place as one of America's foremost modern poets. Over the previous six years, Ezra Pound, H.D., T. S. Eliot, and William Carlos Williams all offered to help her publish a book, but she refused. The world should not allow you to be a recluse, H.D. told Moore when they met one September afternoon in New York. Moore's poems were "greatly superior to what people were making a fuss over" in London, said H.D., "and ought to be known."*

Moore gave them all the same excuse: that her body of work was too slight for a book. The excuse was partly disingenuous—she had more than enough poems each time—and partly strategic. In 1921 H.D. and Bryher brought out Moore's first book, *Poems*, against her explicit objections. This infuriated Moore. She wrote to Bryher, who had financed the publication, that she had considered the matter from every angle and decided that it was not to her "literary advantage" to publish a book just then.† And she was right. Reviews of *Poems* were outright hostile.

Three years later critics greeted *Observations* with enthusiasm. The editors of *The Dial*, the leading literary arts magazine of the 1920s, had persuaded Moore to publish the book so that they could

---

*Reported in Mary Warner Moore to John Warner Moore, September 13, 1920, Rosenbach Museum & Library, Philadelphia. For a full history of the publication of *Observations*, see Robin G. Schulze, ed., *Becoming Marianne Moore: The Early Poems, 1907–1924* (Berkeley: University of California Press, 2002), 18–38; and the author's *Holding On Upside Down: The Life and Work of Marianne Moore* (New York: Farrar, Straus and Giroux, 2013), 179–82, 190–94, 213–22.

†Marianne Moore to Bryher, July 7, 1921, *The Selected Letters of Marianne Moore*, eds. Bonnie Costello with Celeste Goodridge and Cristanne Miller (New York: Knopf, 1997), 164.

surprise her with the annual Dial Award. She was the second poet, after Eliot, to receive this coveted award. It went subsequently to E. E. Cummings, Williams, and Pound. Along with H.D. and Wallace Stevens, these are the modernist poets with whom Moore associated both in person and in print throughout her life. This is the circle of admirers that Herbert S. Gorman referred to when, reviewing *Observations* for *The New York Times*, he wrote that Moore's verse has "long since overgrown the limitations of a coterie." "Certainly no one who possesses a quick interest in contemporary American poetry," he continued, "can afford to remain in ignorance of her sharp, intellectually compact, aristocratic work."[*]

And yet, nearly a century later, too many readers do remain in ignorance of Moore's poetry. She was not peripheral to this coterie. Rather, she was, according to Williams, a "rafter holding up the superstructure of our uncompleted building."[†] Williams and Eliot had little in common aesthetically but shared a deep admiration for Moore. Eliot placed her among the "five contemporary poets— English, Irish, American, French, and German," whose work excited him most.[‡] *Observations* stands with Eliot's *The Waste Land* (1922), Pound's early *Cantos*, Williams's *Spring and All* (1923), and Stevens's *Harmonium* (1923) as one of the landmarks of modernist poetry.

Not since 1925, however, has *Observations* been available to the general reader.[§] Moore cut its fifty-four poems to forty when she assembled her *Selected Poems* in 1935 and cut still more when she put together her *Complete Poems* in 1967. Moore had by then garnered readers from far outside her original circle. Her *Collected Poems* of 1951 received the Pulitzer Prize, the National Book Award, and the Bollingen Prize. With the onset of World War II she distanced herself from her early work because critics had convinced her that

---

[*]Herbert S. Gorman, "Miss Moore's Art Is Not a Democratic One," *New York Times Book Review* (February 1, 1925), BR5.
[†]William Carlos Williams, *Autobiography* (New York: New Directions, 1951), 146.
[‡]T. S. Eliot, review of *Poems* and "Marriage," *The Critical Response to Marianne Moore*, ed. Elizabeth Gregory (Westport, CT: Praeger, 2003), 44.
[§]An invaluable resource for scholars, Schulze's *Becoming Marianne Moore* contains a full facsimile of the first edition of *Observations*.

it was too difficult. Yet in the decades after her death in 1972, Moore's advocates have come to value her modernist work as her greatest achievement.

What was it about Moore's early poetry that so excited her fellow modernists? Initially it was her departure from sentimentality. From the time Moore began writing poems for the Bryn Mawr literary magazine in 1907, the year she turned twenty, she shunned subjects such as "spiritual aspiration, love, and meditation" and preferred instead what she called "critical poetry, the informal Browning kind," because "it is the most impersonal and unforced."* By the time her work came to the attention of other modernists in 1915, she had mastered the art of precision. H.D. called her language "clear, flawless," and "absolutely hard."† However unexpected her word combinations, there is nothing vague or suggestive about them. "With Miss Moore a word is a word most," wrote Williams, "when it is separated out by science, treated with acid to remove the smudges, washed, dried, and placed right side up on a clean surface."‡

She was the first major poet to appropriate for poetry the language of textbooks and commerce. Readers relish her incongruously precise phrases such as "Certain Ming products," "the lion's ferocious chrysanthemum head," and "miniature cavalcades of chlorophylless fungi." Such language strips away the smudges of romance, as when she calls marriage first an "institution" and then an "enterprise," or when she says to the rose, "beauty is a liability."

Over the course of the decade during which she wrote the poems in *Observations*, her precision evolved into more than wit. But so radical were her views that not even her most sympathetic critics at the time tried to interpret them. Twenty-first-century readers may find them more recognizable. To confuse "mushrooms" with "poisonous toadstools" or "mettlesomeness" with "appetite," she writes in "England," is to confess "that one has not looked far

*Marianne Moore to Mary Warner Moore and John Warner Moore, February 22, 1909, Rosenbach Museum & Library.
†H.D., "Marianne Moore," *Critical Response*, 20.
‡William Carlos Williams, "Marianne Moore," *Critical Response*, 72.

enough." In "The Labors of Hercules," it requires a heroically open mind to look beyond racial and national stereotypes. And in "Marriage," Daniel Webster's famous dictum "Liberty and union / Now and forever," discovered on a statue in Central Park, opens the possibility for a domestic union based on individual freedom rather than misconceptions about gender. "An Octopus" similarly celebrates the biodiversity of Mount Rainier National Park as a model for democracy.

To regard people and other living things without stereotypes, without preconceptions, without egocentricity or greed, is for Moore to set them free. "Relentless accuracy," as she calls it in "An Octopus," is her moral and political imperative. Just as the scientist, the critic, and the artist must observe their subjects with precision, so must the citizen and the lover strive to see the other person as an individual. This is for Moore heroic work, an act of love.

Although reviews of *Observations* had little to say about Moore's innovative use of quotations, Scofield Thayer, editor of *The Dial*, privately asked if her quotation marks always referred to another's words or if she ever used them just for emphasis. She had been incorporating quotations and so-called found poems in her work from the time she started writing verse. When she answered that her quotations did come from other sources unless spoken by a character in the poem, he replied that taking them out of their original context enhanced the beauty of the original or, better yet, twisted the original meaning into its opposite.

Unlike the quotations in the *Cantos* and *The Waste Land*, those in *Observations* are not allusions to be recognized by the erudite. When her source is a famous writer such as Tolstoy or Browning, she usually extracts an offhand remark from a diary or a letter rather than from a masterpiece. And she is just as likely to quote a fashion magazine, a newspaper advertisement, or "a comment overheard at the circus" as she is Shakespeare. She was the first of the modernists to use quotations this way and resembles the collage artists of her time who appropriated for their canvases scraps of newspaper, playing cards, and other found objects.

Thayer asked Moore about her quotations after accepting "Sea Unicorns and Land Unicorns" for *The Dial*. He thought he recognized " 'upon her lap,' / its 'mild wild head doth lie.' " Moore answered him with a three-page, single-spaced letter providing sources for all the quotations in the poem. The lines he had taken for a literary allusion were from an anonymous poem in *Punch*, she told him. She disliked the poem except for those lines. He suggested that she include this information in *Observations*, and she decided to annotate all her quotations. She had never added notes to her poems before and painstakingly searched through her notebooks and library for her sources. She thereafter included citations in all her poetry books, though rarely for poems in magazines. The notes not only heighten the irony of her quotations; they also reveal the poet's mind selecting what it needs from the verbal ephemera of modern existence. Her poetry becomes "the self-portrait of a mind," as Glenway Wescott put it, "not as a model and not as beauty, but as experience."*

While Moore's early advocates recognized her craftsmanship— H.D. called her "the perfect technician"†—it took years before critics recognized the originality of her form. Even now Moore's readers may be surprised to learn that, except for her free verse poems of the 1920s, virtually all her poems have a regular pattern of end rhyme. Though Moore prided herself on the originality of her rhymes, they are often so subtle they go unnoticed. Eliot called her "the greatest living master" of "light rhyme" and "the first, so far as I know, who has investigated its possibilities."‡ Sometimes the rhymes are barely audible, as when the preposition *to* rhymes with the first syllable of *superior* in "Those Various Scalpels." And although Moore initially wrote each poem with a complete rhyme scheme, she usually did not repair the pattern when she made revisions. In "Poetry," for instance, the original lines

---

*Glenway Wescott, "Concerning Miss Moore's *Observations*," *Critical Response*, 52.
†H.D., 20.
‡T. S. Eliot, "Introduction to Selected Poems," *Critical Response*, 108.

the immovable critic twitching his skin like a horse that feels
a flea, the base-
ball fan, the statistician—case after case
    could be cited did
    one wish it—nor is it valid*

lose the rhymes of "base-"/"case" and "did"/"valid" when she removed
the superfluous "case after case could be cited did one wish it" for the
first edition of *Observations*.

In 1935 Wallace Stevens became the first critic to point out
that "the units of [Moore's] line are syllables and not feet." He praised
the surprising "effect of ease" produced by the repetition of syllables,
light rhyme, and typographical indentions.† Because of the short
lines, the elements of Moore's stanza are most easily seen in "The
Fish," where each stanza contains six lines of 1-3-8-1-6-9 syllables
and the rhyme scheme is *aaxbbx*.‡ The title, as is often the case with
Moore, serves as the first line.

THE FISH

wade
through black jade.
    Of the crow-blue mussel shells, one
        keeps
        adjusting the ash heaps;
    opening and shutting itself like . . .

Moore always said that she composed in the unit of the stanza
rather than the line. *Observations* reveals her experiments as she
moved from rhymed iambic stanzas to rhymed syllabic ones.

Moore first met other modernist poets and saw modernist
paintings when she visited New York for ten days in December

*Marianne Moore, "Poetry" [1919], *Becoming Marianne Moore*, 205.
†Wallace Stevens, "A Poet That Matters," *Critical Response*, 113–14.
‡Later she converted the poem to five-line stanzas with a rhyme scheme of *aabbx*.

1915.* Although she already knew about imagism and the Armory Show from reading reviews, that trip catalyzed her development as a modernist. She saw how cubist-inspired painters such as Oscar Bluemner and Marsden Hartley liberate the form of their work from its subject matter, how composition, line, color, and the very paint itself exist both independently and in accord with what the painting portrays. Moore's stanza reached maturity the following April. In "Critics and Connoisseurs" she first freed the poem's cadence—or "tune," as she later called it—from the "architecture" of the stanza.† This allowed her poems to have both the natural, irregular rhythms of speech and a formal structure of syllabic rhymed stanzas. Moore's stanza is one of modernism's most underrated achievements.

The pattern of Moore's stanzas often requires that line breaks occur where a reader would not naturally pause—after a preposition, for example, or in the middle of a word. But the punctuation and natural cadence of her sentences, not the line and stanza breaks, determine how the poem should sound. Moore studied prose stylists such as Sir Thomas Browne, Francis Bacon, and Henry James. One of her earliest essays, "The Accented Syllable," points out the pleasure inherent in a dozen prose passages quite apart from their meaning. One should read Moore as one reads Robert Frost, who also imposed what he called "sentence sounds" on a formal structure. Moore's recordings corroborate this, and her revisions over the years show that conciseness and the fluidity of the sentence repeatedly trump the poem's formal pattern.

From 1921 until 1925 Moore abandoned her stanza for free verse. Although she developed her stanza as a modernist alternative

---

*Moore was then living in Carlisle, Pennsylvania, her home since the age of nine. In August 1916 she moved with her mother and brother to Chatham, New Jersey, an hour's train ride from New York City. Two years later, she and her mother moved to Greenwich Village, where she socialized with artists and writers and edited The Dial from 1925 to 1929. She was born in Kirkwood, Missouri, on November 15, 1887, and died in New York City on February 5, 1972.

†"Marianne Moore: The Art of Poetry No. 4," interview by Donald Hall, Paris Review 26 (Summer–Fall 1961), http://www.theparisreview.org/interviews/4637/the-art-of-poetry-no-4 -marianne-moore.

to conventional meter and the formlessness of free verse, she realized that readers grown accustomed to free verse found her line breaks distracting. She even converted several poems initially written in stanzas into free verse. When she resumed writing poetry in 1932, after a seven-year hiatus, she returned to her stanza and never again wrote free verse.

Moore's outrage over the publication of *Poems* made *Observations* a better book. Had *Poems* been "the act of an enemy," Moore said when it appeared, it would be "an attempt to show how little I had accomplished."* She made up for this perceived deficit by writing the longer, more ambitious poems that conclude *Observations*. From 1922 to 1924 she wrote the greatest poem of her career, "An Octopus," along with its companions "Marriage" and "Sea Unicorns and Land Unicorns."

While Moore's refusal to be "poetic" in her language and subject matter thrilled some readers, it vexed others. Reviewers of *Poems* accused Moore of ineptitude with rhyme, meter, and the essential subject matter of poetry: emotion. She was too subtle and original for these critics but felt especially misjudged on the matter of emotion. She thought of herself as deeply emotional, even "Byronesque," as she once described herself in college.† She defended Henry James, with whom she identified, for being "so susceptible to emotion as to be obliged to seem unemotional"‡ and implies the same about James in "An Octopus." Though fond of understatement, Moore would not be underestimated. In "Novices," a response perhaps to *Poems*' reviewers, the novices "write the sort of thing that would in their judgment interest a lady" and fail to recognize in "the detailless perspective of the sea" its torrential power. In "Silence" she introduces a theme to which she would often return: "The deepest feeling always shows itself in silence; / not in silence, but

*Marianne Moore to Robert McAlmon, July 8, 1921, *Selected Letters*, 168.
†Marianne Moore to Mary Warner Moore and John Warner Moore, January 29, 1907, Rosenbach Museum & Library.
‡Marianne Moore, "Feeling and Precision," *The Complete Prose of Marianne Moore*, ed. Patricia C. Willis (New York: Viking, 1986), 401.

restraint." Like the "love that will gaze an eagle blind" in "Marriage," emotions in *Observations* are often violent. In "An Octopus" she describes the "deceptively reserved and flat" glacier atop a volcano. This glacier's lacelike arms "of unimagined delicacy" can kill "prey with the concentric crushing rigor of the python."

There is no such thing as a definitive edition of Moore's poems, for she revised her work throughout her life, continually asserting her authority in an ongoing dialogue with her reader. Most famously, she cut her best-known poem "Poetry" from twenty-nine lines to three in the 1967 *Complete Poems*. Published on her eightieth birthday, *The Complete Poems* presents her final intentions but not necessarily her most compelling ones. Moore was not the same poet at eighty that she had been at thirty-seven, when *Observations* was published, nor was her readership the same. Twenty-first-century readers deserve to know the innovative poems that so excited H.D., Eliot, Williams, Pound, and Stevens and that were an "eye-opener in more ways than one" to the young Elizabeth Bishop.* And they deserve to discover the emotional urgency of this socially engaged poet, whose views about multicultural tolerance, biodiversity, heroic open-mindedness, democracy, and individual liberty we are only now beginning to appreciate.

*Elizabeth Bishop, "Efforts of Affection," *The Collected Prose*, ed. Robert Giroux (New York: Farrar, Straus and Giroux, 1984), 123.

EDITOR'S NOTE

The first edition of *Observations* was released in December 1924 and sold out within a month. Moore prepared a second edition for publication in March 1925. What follows is the entire second edition, plus the two pages from the first edition on which "Poetry" appears. In the second edition Moore substituted for these pages a shorter version of "Poetry" and a new poem, "The Monkey Puzzler." I include "The Monkey Puzzler" and both versions of "Poetry," but otherwise reproduce the second edition because of its numerous corrections to the hastily prepared first edition. Additional typographical errors have been silently corrected and spelling modernized except for that of compound and hyphenated words. Runover lines have been moved flush right, as Moore did herself in the 1960s, to avoid confusion with indented lines. I have not modified Moore's notes and index except to update the punctuation of her citations, to add sources for the 1924 version of "Poetry," and to correct two attributions that Moore changed in later editions of her poems.

Observations

TO AN INTRA-MURAL RAT

You make me think of many men
Once met to be forgot again
   Or merely resurrected
In a parenthesis of wit
That found them hastening through it
   Too brisk to be inspected.

RETICENCE AND VOLUBILITY

"When I am dead,"
The wizard said,
   "I'll look upon the narrow way
   And this Dante,
      And know that he was right
      And he'll delight
         In my remorse,
         Of course."
"When I am dead,"
The student said,
   "I shall have grown so tolerant,
   I'll find I can't
      Laugh at your sorry plight
      Or take delight
         In your chagrin,
         Merlin."

TO A CHAMELEON

Hid by the august foliage and fruit of the grape vine,
Twine
   Your anatomy
     Round the pruned and polished stem,
      Chameleon.
     Fire laid upon
     An emerald as long as
   The Dark King's massy
One,
Could not snap the spectrum up for food as you have done.

A TALISMAN

Under a splintered mast,
Torn from the ship and cast
  Near her hull,

A stumbling shepherd found
Embedded in the ground,
  A seagull

Of lapislazuli,
A scarab of the sea,
  With wings spread—

Curling its coral feet,
Parting its beak to greet
  Men long dead.

TO A PRIZE BIRD

You suit me well, for you can make me laugh,
Nor are you blinded by the chaff
   That every wind sends spinning from the rick.

You know to think, and what you think you speak
With much of Samson's pride and bleak
   Finality; and none dare bid you stop.

Pride sits you well, so strut, colossal bird.
No barnyard makes you look absurd;
   Your brazen claws are staunch against defeat.

INJUDICIOUS GARDENING

If yellow betokens infidelity,
    I am an infidel.
        I could not bear a yellow rose ill will
        Because books said that yellow boded ill,
    White promised well;

However, your particular possession—
    The sense of privacy
        In what you did—deflects from your estate
        Offending eyes, and will not tolerate
    Effrontery.

FEAR IS HOPE

"No man may him hyde
From Deth holow eyed."
   For us two spirits this shall not suffice,
      To whom you are symbolic of a plan
      Concealed within the heart of man.
         Splendid with splendor hid you come, from your Arab
                                       abode,
      An incandescence smothered in the hand of an astrologer
                                   who rode
      Before you, Sun—whom you outran,
      Piercing his caravan.

Sun, you shall stay
With us. Holiday
   And day of wrath shall be as one, wound in a device
      Of Moorish gorgeousness, round glasses spun
      To flame as hemispheres of one
         Great hourglass dwindling to a stem. Consume hostility;
         Employ your weapons in this meeting place of surging
                                     enmity.
      Insurgent feet shall not outrun
      Multiplied flames, O Sun.

TO A STRATEGIST

You brilliant Jew,
You bright particular chameleon, you
　　Regild a shabby fence.

They understood
Your stripes and particolored mind, who could
　　Begrudge you prominence

And call you cold!
But when has prejudice been glad to hold
　　A lizard in its hand—

A subtle thing?
To sense fed on a fine imagining,
　　Sound sense is contraband.

IS YOUR TOWN NINEVEH?

Why so desolate?
  in phantasmagoria about fishes,
    what disgusts you? Could
      not all personal upheaval in
        the name of freedom, be tabooed?

Is it Nineveh
  and are you Jonah
    in the sweltering east wind of your wishes?
      I myself, have stood
        there by the aquarium, looking
          at the Statue of Liberty.

A FOOL, A FOUL THING, A DISTRESSFUL LUNATIC

With webs of cool
    Chain mail and his stout heart, is not the gander
    Mocked, and ignorantly designated yet,
To play the fool?
       "Egyptian vultures clean as cherubim,
    All ivory and jet," are they most foul?
And nature's child,
    That most precocious water bird, the loon—why
    Is he foremost in the madman's alphabet;
Why is he styled
    In folly's catalogue, distressful lunatic?

TO MILITARY PROGRESS

You use your mind
Like a millstone to grind
    Chaff.
You polish it
And with your warped wit
    Laugh

At your torso,
Prostrate where the crow
    Falls
On such faint hearts
As its god imparts,
    Calls

And claps its wings
Till the tumult brings
    More
Black minute-men
To revive again,
    War

At little cost.
They cry for the lost
    Head
And seek their prize
Till the evening sky's
    Red.

AN EGYPTIAN PULLED GLASS BOTTLE
IN THE SHAPE OF A FISH

Here we have thirst
And patience from the first,
    And art, as in a wave held up for us to see
    In its essential perpendicularity;

Not brittle but
Intense—the spectrum, that
    Spectacular and nimble animal the fish,
    Whose scales turn aside the sun's sword with their polish.

TO A STEAM ROLLER

The illustration
is nothing to you without the application.
   You lack half wit. You crush all the particles down
      into close conformity, and then walk back and forth on
                              them.

Sparkling chips of rock
are crushed down to the level of the parent block.
   Were not "impersonal judgment in aesthetic
      matters, a metaphysical impossibility," you

might fairly achieve
it. As for butterflies, I can hardly conceive
   of one's attending upon you, but to question
      the congruence of the complement is vain, if it exists.

DILIGENCE IS TO MAGIC AS PROGRESS IS TO FLIGHT

With an elephant to ride upon—"with rings on her fingers and
                                        bells on her toes,"
    she shall outdistance calamity anywhere she goes.
Speed is not in her mind inseparable from carpets. Locomotion
                                        arose
    in the shape of an elephant; she clambered up and chose
to travel laboriously. So far as magic carpets are concerned, she
                                        knows
    that although the semblance of speed may attach to scarecrows
of aesthetic procedure, the substance of it is embodied in such of
                                        those
    tough-grained animals as have outstripped man's whim to
                                        suppose
them ephemera, and have earned that fruit of their ability to
                                        endure blows,
    which dubs them prosaic necessities—not curios.

TO A SNAIL

If "compression is the first grace of style,"
you have it. Contractility is a virtue
as modesty is a virtue.
It is not the acquisition of any one thing
that is able to adorn,
or the incidental quality that occurs
as a concomitant of something well said,
that we value in style,
but the principle that is hid:
in the absence of feet, "a method of conclusions";
"a knowledge of principles,"
in the curious phenomenon of your occipital horn.

"THE BRICKS ARE FALLEN DOWN, WE WILL BUILD WITH HEWN STONES. THE SYCAMORES ARE CUT DOWN, WE WILL CHANGE TO CEDARS."

In what sense shall we be able to
   secure to ourselves peace and do as they did—
who, when they were not able to rid
   themselves of war, cast out fear?
      They did not say: "We shall not be brought
         into subjection by the naughtiness of the sea;
though we have 'defeated ourselves with
   false balances' and laid weapons in the scale,
glory shall spring from in-glory; hail,
   flood, earthquake, and famine shall
      not intimidate us nor shake the
         foundations of our inalienable energy."

GEORGE MOORE

In speaking of "aspiration,"
    From the recesses of a pen more dolorous than blackness itself,
      Were you presenting us with one more form of imperturbable
                                 French drollery,
         Or was it self directed banter?
         Habitual ennui
               Took from you, your invisible hot helmet of anemia
        While you were filling your little glass from the decanter
        Of a transparent-murky, would-be-truthful
                                 "hobohemia"—
        And then facetiously
        Went off with it? Your soul's supplanter,
    The spirit of good narrative, flatters you, convinced that in
                                reporting briefly
  One choice incident, you have known beauty other than that of
                                     stys, on
Which to fix your admiration.

"NOTHING WILL CURE THE SICK LION
BUT TO EAT AN APE"

Perceiving that in the masked ball
attitude, there is a hollowness
that beauty's light momentum can't redeem,
   since disproportionate satisfaction anywhere
   lacks a proportionate air,

he let us know without offense
by his hands' denunciatory
upheaval, that he despised the fashion
   of curing us with an ape—making it his care
   to smother us with fresh air.

TO THE PEACOCK OF FRANCE

In "taking charge of your possessions when you saw them," you
                              became a golden jay.
Scaramouche said you charmed his charm away,
  But not his color? Yes, his color when you liked.
Of chiseled setting and black-opalescent dye,
  You were the jewelry of sense;
    Of sense, not license; you but trod the pace
    Of liberty in market-place
      And court. Molière,
      The huggermugger repertory of your first adventure,
                              is your own affair.

"Anchorites do not dwell in theatres," and peacocks do not
                              flourish in a cell.
Why make distinctions? The results were well
  When you were on the boards; nor were your triumphs bought
At horrifying sacrifice of stringency.
    You hated sham; you ranted up
      And down through the conventions of excess;
      Nor did the King love you the less
        Nor did the world,
        In whose chief interest and for whose spontaneous
                              delight, your broad tail was unfurled.

IN THIS AGE OF HARD TRYING,
NONCHALANCE IS GOOD AND

"Really, it is not the
    business of the gods to bake clay pots." They need not
        do it in this instance. A few
           revolved upon the axes of their worth
    as if excessive popularity might be a pot;

they did not venture the
    profession of humility. The polished wedge
        that might have split the firmament
           was dumb. At last it threw itself away
    and falling down, conferred on some poor fool, a privilege.

"Taller by the length of
    a conversation of five hundred years than all
        the others," there was one, whose tales
           of what could never have been actual—
    were better than the haggish, uncompanionable drawl

of certitude; his by-
    play was more terrible in its effectiveness
        than the fiercest frontal attack.
           The staff, the bag, the feigned inconsequence
of manner, best bespeak that weapon, self protectiveness.

TO STATECRAFT EMBALMED

"There is nothing to be said for you. Guard
Your secret. Conceal it under your hard
   Plumage, necromancer.
     O
Bird, whose tents were "awnings of Egyptian
Yarn," shall Justice' faint, zigzag inscription—
   Leaning like a dancer—
     Show
The pulse of its once vivid sovereignty?
You say not, and transmigrating from the
   Sarcophagus, you wind
     Snow
Silence round us and with moribund talk,
Half limping and half ladified, you stalk
   About. Ibis, we find
     No
Virtue in you—alive and yet so dumb.
Discreet behavior is not now the sum
   Of statesmanlike good sense.
     Though
It were the incarnation of dead grace?
As if a death mask ever could replace
   Life's faulty excellence!
     Slow
To remark the steep, too strict proportion
Of your throne, you'll see the wrenched distortion
   Of suicidal dreams
     Go

Staggering toward itself and with its bill,
Attack its own identity, until
   Foe seems friend and friend seems
     Foe.

THE MONKEY PUZZLER

A kind of monkey or pine-lemur
not of interest to the monkey,
but to the animal higher up which resembles it,
in a kind of Flaubert's Carthage, it defies one—
this "Paduan cat with lizard," this "tiger in a bamboo thicket."
"An interwoven somewhat," it will not come out.
Ignore the Foo dog and it is forthwith more than a dog,
its tail superimposed upon itself in a complacent half spiral,
incidentally so witty;
but this pine-tree—this pine-tiger, is a tiger, not a dog.
It knows that if a nomad may have dignity,
Gibraltar has had more—
that "it is better to be lonely than unhappy."
A conifer contrived in imitation of the glyptic work of jade and
                                        hard stone cutters,
a true curio in this bypath of curio collecting,
it is worth its weight in gold but no one takes it
from these woods in which society's not knowing is colossal,
the lion's ferocious chrysanthemum head seeming kind in
                                        comparison.
This porcupine-quilled, infinitely complicated starkness—
this is beauty—"a certain proportion in the skeleton which gives
                                        the best results."
One is at a loss, however, to know why it should be here,
in this morose part of the earth—
to account for its origin at all;
but we prove, we do not explain our birth.

POETRY [1924]

I too, dislike it: there are things that are important beyond all this
                                                          fiddle.
   Reading it, however, with a perfect contempt for it, one
                                                discovers that there is in
   it after all, a place for the genuine.
     Hands that can grasp, eyes
    that can dilate, hair that can rise
      if it must, these things are important not because a

high sounding interpretation can be put upon them but because
                                                          they are
   useful; when they become so derivative as to become
                                                unintelligible,
   the same thing may be said for all of us, that we
    do not admire what
    we cannot understand: the bat,
      holding on upside down or in quest of something to

eat, elephants pushing, a wild horse taking a roll, a tireless wolf
                                                          under
   a tree, the immovable critic twitching his skin like a horse that
                                                feels a flea, the base-
   ball fan, the statistician—
    nor is it valid
     to discriminate against "business documents and

school-books"; all these phenomena are important. One must
                                                make a distinction

however: when dragged into prominence by half poets, the
result is not poetry,
nor till the poets among us can be
"literalists of
the imagination"—above
insolence and triviality and can present

for inspection, imaginary gardens with real toads in them, shall
we have
it. In the meantime, if you demand on one hand,
the raw material of poetry in
all its rawness and
that which is on the other hand
genuine, then you are interested in poetry.

POETRY [1925]

I too, dislike it:
there are things that are important beyond all this fiddle.
The bat, upside down; the elephant pushing,
a tireless wolf under a tree,
the base-ball fan, the statistician—
"business documents and schoolbooks"—
these phenomena are pleasing,
but when they have been fashioned
into that which is unknowable,
we are not entertained.
It may be said of all of us
that we do not admire what we cannot understand;
enigmas are not poetry.

THE PAST IS THE PRESENT

If external action is effete
   and rhyme is outmoded,
      I shall revert to you,
      Habakkuk, as on a recent occasion I was goaded
         into doing, by XY, who was speaking of unrhymed verse.
This man said—I think that I repeat
   his identical words:
      "Hebrew poetry is
   prose with a sort of heightened consciousness. 'Ecstasy affords
      the occasion and expediency determines the form.'"

PEDANTIC LITERALIST

Prince Rupert's drop, paper muslin ghost,
   White torch—"with power to say unkind
Things with kindness, and the most
     Irritating things in the midst of love and
      Tears," you invite destruction.

You are like the meditative man
   With the perfunctory heart; its
Carved cordiality ran
     To and fro at first like an inlaid and royal
      Immutable production;

Then afterward "neglected to be
   Painful, deluding him with
Loitering formality,"
     "Doing its duty as if it did it not,"
      Presenting an obstruction

To the motive that it served. What stood
   Erect in you has withered. A
Little "palm tree of turned wood"
     Informs your once spontaneous core in its
      Immutable production.

"HE WROTE THE HISTORY BOOK"

There! You shed a ray
    of whimsicality on a mask of profundity so
        terrific, that I have been dumbfounded by
it oftener than I care to say.
        The book? Titles are chaff.

Authentically
    brief and full of energy, you contribute to your father's
        legibility and are sufficiently
synthetic. Thank you for showing me
        your father's autograph.

CRITICS AND CONNOISSEURS

There is a great amount of poetry in unconscious
    fastidiousness. Certain Ming
        products, imperial floor coverings of coach
    wheel yellow, are well enough in their way but I have seen
                                something
            that I like better—a
                mere childish attempt to make an imperfectly ballasted
                            animal stand up,
                similar determination to make a pup
                eat his meat on the plate.

I remember a swan under the willows in Oxford
    with flamingo colored, maple-
        leaflike fleet. It reconnoitered like a battle
    ship. Disbelief and conscious fastidiousness were the staple
            ingredients in its
                disinclination to move. Finally its hardihood was not
                            proof against its
                proclivity to more fully appraise such bits
                of food as the stream

bore counter to it; it made away with what I gave it
    to eat. I have seen this swan and
        I have seen you; I have seen ambition without
    understanding in a variety of forms. Happening to stand
            by an ant hill, I have
                seen a fastidious ant carrying a stick, north, south, east,
                            west, till it turned on

itself, struck out from the flower bed into the lawn,
        and returned to the point

from which it had started. Then abandoning the stick as
    useless and overtaxing its
        jaws with a particle of whitewash pill-like but
    heavy, it again went through the same course of procedure.
                                                        What is
            there in being able
                to say that one has dominated the stream in an attitude
                                            of self defense,
                in proving that one has had the experience
                    of carrying a stick?

TO BE LIKED BY YOU WOULD BE A CALAMITY

"Attack is more piquant than concord," but when
   You tell me frankly that you would like to feel
      My flesh beneath your feet,
         I'm all abroad; I can but put my weapon up, and
           Bow you out.
Gesticulation—it is half the language.
   Let unsheathed gesticulation be the steel
      Your courtesy must meet,
         Since in your hearing words are mute, which to my senses
           Are a shout.

LIKE A BULRUSH

or the spike
of a channel marker or the
moon, he superintended the demolition of his image in
the water by the wind; he did not strike

them at the
time as being different from
any other inhabitant of the water; it was as if he
were a seal in the combined livery

of bird plus
snake; it was as if he knew that
the penguins were not fish and as if in their bat blindness, they
                                                                    did not
realize that he was amphibious.

SOJOURN IN THE WHALE

Trying to open locked doors with a sword, threading
   the points of needles, planting shade trees
   upside down; swallowed by the opaqueness of one whom the
                                         seas
love better than they love you, Ireland—

you have lived and lived on every kind of shortage.
   You have been compelled by hags to spin
   gold thread from straw and have heard men say: "There is a
                                     feminine
temperament in direct contrast to

ours which makes her do these things. Circumscribed by a
   heritage of blindness and native
   incompetence, she will become wise and will be forced to give
in. Compelled by experience, she

will turn back; water seeks its own level": and you
   have smiled. "Water in motion is far
   from level." You have seen it when obstacles happened to bar
the path—rise automatically.

MY APISH COUSINS

winked too much and were afraid of snakes. The zebras,
                                                    supreme in
their abnormality; the elephants with their fog-colored skin
    and strictly practical appendages
        were there, the small cats; and the parakeet—
            trivial and humdrum on examination, destroying
            bark and portions of the food it could not eat.

I recall their magnificence, now not more magnificent
than it is dim. It is difficult to recall the ornament,
    speech, and precise manner of what one might
        call the minor acquaintances twenty
            years back; but I shall not forget him—that Gilgamesh
                                                    among
        the hairy carnivora—that cat with the

wedge-shaped, slate-gray marks on its forelegs and the resolute
                                                    tail,
astringently remarking: "They have imposed on us with their
                                                    pale
    half fledged protestations, trembling about
        in inarticulate frenzy, saying
            it is not for us to understand art; finding it
            all so difficult, examining the thing

as if it were inconceivably arcanic, as symmet-
rically frigid as if it had been carved out of chrysoprase

or marble—strict with tension, malignant
    in its power over us and deeper
        than the sea when it proffers flattery in exchange for
                                  hemp,
  rye, flax, horses, platinum, timber, and fur."

ROSES ONLY

You do not seem to realize that beauty is a liability rather than
an asset—that in view of the fact that spirit creates form we are
                                        justified in supposing
        that you must have brains. For you, a symbol of the unit,
                                        stiff and sharp,
conscious of surpassing by dint of native superiority and liking
                                        for everything
self-dependent, anything an

ambitious civilization might produce: for you, unaided to attempt
                                        through sheer
        reserve, to confute presumptions resulting from observation, is
                                        idle. You cannot make us
        think you a delightful happen-so. But rose, if you are
                                        brilliant, it
is not because your petals are the without-which-nothing of
                                        pre-eminence. You would, minus thorns,
look like a what-is-this, a mere

peculiarity. They are not proof against a worm, the elements, or
                                        mildew
        but what about the predatory hand? What is brilliance without
                                        co-ordination? Guarding the
        infinitesimal pieces of your mind, compelling audience to
        the remark that it is better to be forgotten than to be
                                        remembered too violently,
your thorns are the best part of you.

REINFORCEMENTS

The vestibule to experience is not to
    be exalted into epic grandeur. These men are going
to their work with this idea, advancing like a school of fish
                                through

still water—waiting to change the course or dismiss
    the idea of movement, till forced to. The words of the Greeks
ring in our ears, but they are vain in comparison with a sight
                                like this.

The pulse of intention does not move so that one
    can see it, and moral machinery is not labeled, but
the future of time is determined by the power of volition.

THE FISH

wade
through black jade.
    Of the crow-blue mussel shells, one
        keeps
        adjusting the ash heaps;
    opening and shutting itself like

an
injured fan.
    The barnacles which encrust the
        side
        of the wave, cannot hide
    there for the submerged shafts of the

sun,
split like spun
    glass, move themselves with spotlight swift-
        ness
        into the crevices—
    in and out, illuminating

the
turquoise sea
    of bodies. The water drives a
        wedge
        of iron through the iron edge
    of the cliff, whereupon the stars,

pink
rice grains, ink
    bespattered jelly-fish, crabs like
      green
      lilies and submarine
    toadstools, slide each on the other.

All
external
    marks of abuse are present on
      this
      defiant edifice—
    all the physical features of

ac-
cident—lack
    of cornice, dynamite grooves, burns
      and
      hatchet strokes, these things stand
    out on it; the chasm side is

dead.
Repeated
    evidence has proved that it can
      live
      on what cannot revive
    its youth. The sea grows old in it.

BLACK EARTH

Openly, yes,
with the naturalness
   of the hippopotamus or the alligator
   when it climbs out on the bank to experience the

sun, I do these
things which I do, which please
   no one but myself. Now I breathe and now I am sub-
   merged; the blemishes stand up and shout when the object

in view was a
renaissance; shall I say
   the contrary? The sediment of the river which
   encrusts my joints, makes me very gray but I am used

to it, it may
remain there; do away
   with it and I am myself done away with, for the
   patina of circumstance can but enrich what was

there to begin
with. This elephant skin
   which I inhabit, fibered over like the shell of
   the coconut, this piece of black glass through which no light

can filter—cut
into checkers by rut
   upon rut of unpreventable experience—
   it is a manual for the peanut-tongued and the

hairy toed. Black
but beautiful, my back
    is full of the history of power. Of power? What
    is powerful and what is not? My soul shall never

be cut into
by a wooden spear; through-
    out childhood to the present time, the unity of
    life and death has been expressed by the circumference

described by my
trunk; nevertheless, I
    perceive feats of strength to be inexplicable after
    all; and I am on my guard; external poise, it

has its center
well nurtured—we know
    where—in pride, but spiritual poise, it has its center where?
    My ears are sensitized to more than the sound of

the wind. I see
and I hear, unlike the
    wandlike body of which one hears so much, which was made
    to see and not to see; to hear and not to hear;

that tree trunk without
roots, accustomed to shout
    its own thoughts to itself like a shell, maintained intact
    by one who knows what strange pressure of the atmosphere;
                                              that

spiritual
brother to the coral
    plant, absorbed into which, the equable sapphire light
    becomes a nebulous green. The I of each is to

the I of each,
a kind of fretful speech
    which sets a limit on itself; the elephant is?
    Black earth preceded by a tendril? It is to that

phenomenon
the above formation,
    translucent like the atmosphere—a cortex merely—
    that on which darts cannot strike decisively the first

time, a substance
needful as an instance
    of the indestructibility of matter; it
    has looked at the electricity and at the earth-

quake and is still
here; the name means thick. Will
    depth be depth, thick skin be thick, to one who can see no
    beautiful element of unreason under it?

RADICAL

Tapering
to a point, conserving everything,
   this carrot is predestined to be thick.
      The world is
      but a circumstance, a mis-
         erable corn-patch for its feet. With ambition, imagination,
                         outgrowth,

nutriment,
with everything crammed belligerent-
   ly inside itself, its fibers breed mon-
      opoly—
      a tail-like, wedge-shaped engine with the
         secret of expansion, fused with intensive heat to the color
                       of the set-

ting sun and
stiff. For the man in the straw hat, stand-
   ing still and turning to look back at it,
      as much as
      to say my happiest moment has
         been funereal in comparison with this, the conditions of
                       life pre-

determined
slavery to be easy and freedom hard. For
   it? Dismiss
   agrarian lore; it tells him this:
      that which it is impossible to force, it is impossible to hinder.

IN THE DAYS OF PRISMATIC COLOR

not in the days of Adam and Eve but when Adam
    was alone; when there was no smoke and color was
fine, not with the fineness of
    early civilization art but by virtue
of its originality; with nothing to modify it but the

mist that went up, obliqueness was a varia-
    tion of the perpendicular, plain to see and
to account for: it is no
    longer that; nor did the blue red yellow band
of incandescence that was color keep its stripe: it also is one of

those things into which much that is peculiar can be
    read; complexity is not a crime but carry
it to the point of murki-
    ness and nothing is plain. Complexity
moreover, that has been committed to darkness, instead of
                            granting it-

self to be the pestilence that it is, moves all a-
    bout as if to bewilder us with the dismal
fallacy that insistence
    is the measure of achievement and that all
truth must be dark. Principally throat, sophistication is as it al-

ways has been—at the antipodes from the init-
    ial great truths. "Part of it was crawling, part of it
was about to crawl, the rest

was torpid in its lair." In the short legged, fit-
ful advance, the gurgling and all the minutiae—we have the
                                                    classic

multitude of feet. To what purpose! Truth is no Apollo
    Belvedere, no formal thing. The wave may go over it if it likes.
Know that it will be there when it says:
    "I shall be there when the wave has gone by."

PETER

Strong and slippery, built for the midnight grass-party confronted
                                          by four cats,
    he sleeps his time away—the detached first claw on his foreleg
                                  which corresponds
        to the thumb, retracted to its tip; the small tuft of fronds
            or katydid legs above each eye, still numbering the units in
                                          each group;
            the shadbones regularly set about his mouth, to droop or
                                              rise

in unison like the porcupine's quills—motionless. He lets himself
                                          be flat-
    tened out by gravity, as it were a piece of seaweed tamed and
                                  weakened by
        exposure to the sun; compelled when extended, to lie
            stationary. Sleep is the result of his delusion that one must
                                              do as
        well as one can for oneself; sleep—epitome of what is to

him as to the average person, the end of life. Demonstrate on him
                                          how
    the lady caught the dangerous southern snake, placing a forked
                                  stick on either
        side of its innocuous neck; one need not try to stir
            him up; his prune shaped head and alligator eyes are not a
                                      party to the
        joke. Lifted and handled, he may be dangled like an eel
                                      or set

up on the forearm like a mouse; his eyes bisected by pupils of a

                                         pin's

  width, are flickeringly exhibited, then covered up. May be? I

                                       should say,

    might have been; when he has been got the better of in a

    dream—as in a fight with nature or with cats—we all

                              know it. Profound sleep is

      not with him, a fixed illusion. Springing about with

                            froglike ac-

curacy, emitting jerky cries when taken in the hand, he is himself

  again; to sit caged by the rungs of a domestic chair would be

                              unprofit-

  able—human. What is the good of hypocrisy? It

    is permissible to choose one's employment, to abandon the

                         wire nail, the

    roly-poly, when it shows signs of being no longer a pleas-

ure, to score the adjacent magazine with a double line of strokes.

                               He can

  talk, but insolently says nothing. What of it? When one is

                         frank, one's very

  presence is a compliment. It is clear that he can see

    the virtue of naturalness, that he is one of those who do not

                           regard

    the published fact as a surrender. As for the disposition

invariably to affront, an animal with claws wants to have to use

  them; that eel-like extension of trunk into tail is not an

                           accident. To

  leap, to lengthen out, divide the air—to purloin, to pursue,

    to tell the hen: fly over the fence, go in the wrong way—in

                       your perturba-

  tion—this is life; to do less would be nothing but

                         dishonesty.

DOCK RATS

There are human beings who seem to regard the place as craftily
as we do—who seem to feel that it is a good place to come
home to. On what a river; wide—twinkling like a chopped sea
                                                under some
    of the finest shipping in the

world: the square-rigged Flemish four-master, the liner, the
                                battleship like the two-
        thirds submerged section of an iceberg; the tug
        dipping and pushing, the bell striking as it comes; the steam
                                                yacht, lying
            like a new made arrow on the

stream; the ferry-boat—a head assigned, one to each
                                    compartment, making
        a row of chessmen set for play. When the wind is from the
                                                east,
        the smell is of apples, of hay; the aroma increased and
                                                decreased
            as the wind changes;

of rope, of mountain leaves for florists; as from the west,
        it is aromatic of salt. Occasionally a parakeet
        from Brazil, arrives clasping and clawing; or a monkey—tail
                                                and feet
            in readiness for an over-

ture; all arms and tail; how delightful! There is the sea, moving
                                                    the bulk-
    head with its horse strength; and the multiplicity of rudders
    and propellers; the signals, shrill, questioning, peremptory,
                                                    diverse;
        the wharf cats and the barge dogs; it

is easy to overestimate the value of such things. One does
    not live in such a place from motives of expediency
    but because to one who has been accustomed to it, shipping is
                                                    the
        most interesting thing in the world.

PICKING AND CHOOSING

Literature is a phase of life: if
     one is afraid of it, the situation is irremediable; if
one approaches it familiarly,
     what one says of it is worthless. Words are constructive
when they are true; the opaque allusion—the simulated flight

upward—accomplishes nothing. Why cloud the fact
     that Shaw is selfconscious in the field of sentiment but is
                                   otherwise re-
warding? that James is all that has been
     said of him, if *feeling* is profound? It is not Hardy
the distinguished novelist and Hardy the poet, but one man

"interpreting life through the medium of the
     emotions." If he must give an opinion, it is permissible that the
critic should know what he likes. Gordon
     Craig with his "this is I" and "this is mine," with his three
wise men, his "sad French greens" and his Chinese cherries—
                                   Gordon Craig, so

inclinational and unashamed—has carried
     the precept of being a good critic, to the last extreme; and
                                   Burke is a
psychologist—of acute, raccoon-
     like curiosity. *Summa diligentia*;
to the humbug, whose name is so amusing—very young and ve-

ry rushed, Caesar crossed the Alps on the "top of a
   diligence." We are not daft about the meaning but this
                                                    familiarity
with wrong meanings puzzles one. Humming-
   bug, the candles are not wired for electricity.
Small dog, going over the lawn, nipping the linen and saying

that you have a badger—remember Xenophon;
   only the most rudimentary sort of behavior is necessary
to put us on the scent; "a right good
   salvo of barks," a few "strong wrinkles" puckering the
skin between the ears, are all we ask.

ENGLAND

with its baby rivers and little towns, each with its abbey or its
                                              cathedral,
     with voices—one voice perhaps, echoing through the
                                        transept—the
criterion of suitability and convenience: and Italy with its equal
     shores—contriving an epicureanism from which the
                                        grossness has been

extracted: and Greece with its goats and its gourds, the nest of
                                        modified illusions:
     and France, the "chrysalis of the nocturnal butterfly" in
whose products, mystery of construction diverts one from what
                                        was originally one's
     object—substance at the core: and the East with its snails,
                                        its emotional

shorthand and jade cockroaches, its rock crystal and its
                                        imperturbability,
     all of museum quality; and America where there
is the little old ramshackle victoria in the south, where cigars are
                                        smoked on the
     street in the north; where there are no proof readers, no
                                        silkworms, no digressions;

the wild man's land; grass-less, links-less, language-less country
                                        in which letters are written
     not in Spanish, not in Greek, not in Latin, not in shorthand

but in plain American which cats and dogs can read! The letter
                    "a" in psalm and calm when
          pronounced with the sound of "a" in candle, is very
                              noticeable but

why should continents of misapprehension have to be accounted
                              for by the
     fact? Does it follow that because there are poisonous toadstools
which resemble mushrooms, both are dangerous? In the case of
                         mettlesomeness which may be
          mistaken for appetite, of heat which may appear to be
                              haste, no con-

clusions may be drawn. To have misapprehended the matter, is to
                              have confessed
     that one has not looked far enough. The sublimated wisdom
of China, Egyptian discernment, the cataclysmic torrent of
                         emotion compressed
          in the verbs of the Hebrew language, the books of the man
                              who is able

to say, "I envy nobody but him and him only, who catches more
                              fish than
     I do"—the flower and fruit of all that noted superi-
ority—should one not have stumbled upon it in America, must
                              one imagine
          that it is not there? It has never been confined to one
                              locality.

WHEN I BUY PICTURES

or what is closer to the truth,
when I look at that of which I may regard myself as the
                                    imaginary possessor,
I fix upon what would give me pleasure in my average moments:
the satire upon curiosity in which no more is discernible than
the intensity of the mood;
or quite the opposite—the old thing, the medieval decorated
                                    hat-box,
in which there are hounds with waists diminishing like the waist
                                    of the hourglass
and deer and birds and seated people;
it may be no more than a square of parquetry; the literal
                                    biography perhaps,
in letters standing well apart upon a parchment-like expanse;
an artichoke in six varieties of blue; the snipe-legged hieroglyphic
                                    in three parts;
the silver fence protecting Adam's grave, or Michael taking
                                    Adam by the wrist.
Too stern an intellectual emphasis upon this quality or that,
                                    detracts from one's enjoyment;
it must not wish to disarm anything; nor may the approved
                                    triumph easily be honored—
that which is great because something else is small.
It comes to this: of whatever sort it is,
it must be "lit with piercing glances into the life of things";
it must acknowledge the spiritual forces which have made it.

A GRAVE

Man looking into the sea,
taking the view from those who have as much right to it as you
                                have to it yourself,
it is human nature to stand in the middle of a thing
but you cannot stand in the middle of this:
the sea has nothing to give but a well excavated grave.
The firs stand in a procession, each with an emerald turkey-foot
                                at the top,
reserved as their contours, saying nothing;
repression, however, is not the most obvious characteristic of the
                                sea;
the sea is a collector, quick to return a rapacious look.
There are others besides you who have worn that look—
whose expression is no longer a protest; the fish no longer
                                investigate them
for their bones have not lasted:
men lower nets, unconscious of the fact that they are desecrating
                                a grave,
and row quickly away—the blades of the oars
moving together like the feet of water-spiders as if there were no
                                such thing as death.
The wrinkles progress upon themselves in a phalanx—beautiful
                                under networks of foam,
and fade breathlessly while the sea rustles in and out of the
                                seaweed;
the birds swim through the air at top speed, emitting cat-calls as
                                heretofore—

the tortoise-shell scourges about the feet of the cliffs, in motion
                                                beneath them
and the ocean, under the pulsation of lighthouse and noise of
                                                bell-buoys,
advances as usual, looking as if it were not that ocean in which
                        dropped things are bound to sink—
in which if they turn and twist, it is neither with volition nor
                                        consciousness.

THOSE VARIOUS SCALPELS

those
various sounds consistently indistinct, like intermingled echoes
    struck from thin glasses successively at random—the
    inflection disguised: your hair, the tails of two fighting-cocks
              head to head in stone—like sculptured scimitars re-
    peating the curve of your ears in reverse order: your eyes,
                               flowers of ice

and
snow sown by tearing winds on the cordage of disabled ships:
                             your raised hand
    an ambiguous signature: your cheeks, those rosettes
    of blood on the stone floors of French châteaux, with regard to
                which the guides are so affirmative:
      your other hand

a
bundle of lances all alike, partly hid by emeralds from Persia
    and the fractional magnificence of Florentine
    goldwork—a collection of half a dozen little objects made fine
      with enamel in gray, yellow, and dragon fly blue; a lemon, a

pear
and three bunches of grapes, tied with silver: your dress, a
                      magnificent square
      cathedral of uniform
      and at the same time, diverse appearance—a species of vertical
                   vineyard rustling in the storm

of conventional opinion. Are they weapons or scalpels?
                                                    Whetted

to
brilliance by the hard majesty of that sophistication which is su-
    perior to opportunity, these things are rich
        instruments with which to experiment but surgery is not
                    tentative. Why dissect destiny with instruments which
            are more highly specialized than the tissues of destiny itself?

THE LABORS OF HERCULES

To popularize the mule, its neat exterior
expressing the principle of accommodation reduced to a
                                        minimum:
to persuade one of austere taste, proud in the possession of home,
                                        and a musician—
that the piano is a free field for etching; that his "charming
                                        tadpole notes"
belong to the past when one had time to play them:
to persuade those self-wrought Midases of brains
whose fourteen-karat ignorance aspires to rise in value
"till the sky is the limit,"
that excessive conduct augurs disappointment,
that one must not borrow a long white beard and tie it on
and threaten with the scythe of time, the casually curious:
to teach the bard with too elastic a selectiveness
that one detects creative power by its capacity to conquer one's
                                        detachment;
that while it may have more elasticity than logic,
it knows where it is going;
it flies along in a straight line like electricity
depopulating areas that boast of their remoteness:
to prove to the high priests of caste
that snobbishness is a stupidity,
the best side out, of age-old toadyism,
kissing the feet of the man above,
kicking the face of the man below:
to teach the patron-saints-to-atheists, the Coliseum
meet-me-alone-by-moonlight maudlin troubadour

that kickups for catstrings are not life
nor yet appropriate to death—that we are sick of the earth,
sick of the pig-sty, wild geese and wild men:
to convince snake-charming controversialists
that it is one thing to change one's mind,
another to eradicate it—that one keeps on knowing
"that the Negro is not brutal.
that the Jew is not greedy,
that the Oriental is not immoral,
that the German is not a Hun."

NEW YORK

the savage's romance,
accreted where we need the space for commerce—
the center of the wholesale fur trade,
starred with tepees of ermine and peopled with foxes,
the long guard-hairs waving two inches beyond the body of the pelt;
the ground dotted with deer-skins—white with white spots
"as satin needlework in a single color may carry a varied pattern,"
and wilting eagles' down compacted by the wind;
and picardels of beaver skin; white ones alert with snow.
It is a far cry from the "queen full of jewels"
and the beau with the muff,
from the gilt coach shaped like a perfume bottle,
to the conjunction of the Monongahela and the Allegheny,
and the scholastic philosophy of the wilderness
to combat which one must stand outside and laugh
since to go in is to be lost.
It is not the dime-novel exterior,
Niagara Falls, the calico horses and the war canoe;
it is not that "if the fur is not finer than such as one sees others wear,
one would rather be without it—"
that estimated in raw meat and berries, we could feed the
                                                        universe;

it is not the atmosphere of ingenuity,
the otter, the beaver, the puma skins
without shooting-irons or dogs;
it is not the plunder,
it is the "accessibility to experience."

PEOPLE'S SURROUNDINGS

they answer one's questions:
a deal table compact with the wall;
in this dried bone of arrangement,
one's "natural promptness" is compressed, not crowded out;
one's style is not lost in such simplicity:

the palace furniture, so old fashioned, so old fashionable;
Sèvres china and the fireplace dogs—
bronze dromios with pointed ears, as obsolete as pugs;
one has one's preference in the matter of bad furniture
and this is not one's choice:

the vast indestructible necropolis
of composite Yawman-Erbe separable units;
the steel, the oak, the glass, the Poor Richard publications
containing the public secrets of efficiency
on "paper so thin that one thousand four hundred and twenty
                                    pages make one inch,"
exclaiming so to speak, When you take my time, you take
                              something I had meant to use:

the highway hid by fir trees in rhododendron twenty feet deep,
the peacocks, hand-forged gates, old Persian velvet—
roses outlined in pale black on an ivory ground—
the pierced iron shadows of the cedars,
Chinese carved glass, old Waterford,
lettered ladies; landscape gardening twisted into permanence:

straight lines over such great distances as one finds in Utah or in
                                                                    Texas
where people do not have to be told
that "a good brake is as important as a good motor,"
where by means of extra sense cells in the skin,
they can like trout, smell what is coming—
those cool sirs with the explicit sensory apparatus of common
                                                                    sense,
who know the exact distance between two points as the crow
                                                                    flies;
there is something attractive about a mind that moves in a
                                                    straight line—
the municipal bat-roost of mosquito warfare, concrete statuary,
medicaments for "instant beauty" in the hands of all,
and that live wire, the American string quartet:

and Bluebeard's tower above the coral reefs,
the magic mousetrap closing on all points of the compass,
capping like petrified surf, the furious azure of the bay
where there is no dust and life is like a lemon-leaf,
a green piece of tough translucent parchment,
where the crimson, the copper, and the Chinese vermilion of the
                                                                    poincianas
set fire to the masonry and turquoise blues refute the clock;
this dungeon with odd notions of hospitality,
with its "chessmen carved out of moonstones,"
its mocking-birds, fringed lilies, and hibiscus,
its black butterflies with blue half circles on their wings,
tan goats with onyx ears, its lizards glittering and without
                                                                    thickness
like splashes of fire and silver on the pierced turquoise of the
                                                                    lattices
and the acacia-like lady shivering at the touch of a hand,
lost in a small collision of the orchids—
dyed quicksilver let fall

to disappear like an obedient chameleon in fifty shades of mauve
                                     and amethyst:
here where the mind of this establishment has come to the
                                     conclusion
that it would be impossible to revolve about one's self too much,
sophistication has like "an escalator, cut the nerve of progress."

In these noncommittal, personal-impersonal expressions of
                                     appearance,
the eye knows what to skip;
the physiognomy of conduct must not reveal the skeleton;
"a setting must not have the air of being one"
yet with x-raylike inquisitive intensity upon it, the surfaces go
                                     back;
the interfering fringes of expression are but a stain on what
                                     stands out,
there is neither up nor down to it;
we see the exterior and the fundamental structure—
captains of armies, cooks, carpenters,
cutlers, gamesters, surgeons and armorers,
lapidaries, silkmen, glovers, fiddlers and ballad-singers,
sextons of churches, dyers of black cloth, hostlers and chimney-
                                     sweeps,
queens, countesses, ladies, emperors, travelers and mariners,
dukes, princes and gentlemen
in their respective places—
camps, forges and battlefields,
conventions, oratories and wardrobes,
dens, deserts, railway stations, asylums and places where engines
                                     are made,
shops, prisons, brickyards and altars of churches—
in magnificent places clean and decent,
castles, palaces, dining-halls, theaters and imperial audience-
                                     chambers.

SNAKES, MONGOOSES, SNAKE-CHARMERS, AND THE LIKE

I have a friend who would give a price for those long fingers all
                        of one length—
those hideous bird's claws, for that exotic asp and the
                            mongoose—
products of the country in which everything is hard work, the
                   country of the grass-getter,
the torch-bearer, the dog-servant, the message-bearer, the holy-man.
Engrossed in this distinguished worm nearly as wild and as fierce
                   as the day it was captured,
he gazes as if incapable of looking at anything with a view to
                           analysis.
"The slight snake rippling quickly through the grass,
the leisurely tortoise with its pied back,
the chameleon passing from twig to stone, from stone to straw,"
lit his imagination at one time; his admiration now converges
                          upon this:
thick, not heavy, it stands up from its traveling-basket,
the essentially Greek, the plastic animal, all of a piece from nose
                           to tail;
one is compelled to look at it as at the shadows of the alps
imprisoning in their folds like flies in amber, the rhythms of the
                       skating-rink.
This animal to which from the earliest times, importance has
                         attached,
fine as its worshippers have said—for what was it invented?
To show that when intelligence in its pure form
has embarked on a train of thought which is unproductive, it will
                       come back?

We do not know; the only positive thing about it is its shape, but
                                              why protest?
The passion for setting people right is in itself an afflictive
                                              disease.
Distaste which takes no credit to itself is best.

BOWLS

on the green
with lignum vitae balls and ivory markers,
the pins planted in wild duck formation,
and quickly dispersed:
by this survival of ancient punctilio
in the manner of Chinese lacquer carving,
layer after layer exposed by certainty of touch and unhurried
                                                        incision
so that only so much color shall be revealed as is necessary to the
                                                        picture
I learn that we are precisians—
not citizens of Pompeii arrested in action
as a cross section of one's correspondence would seem to imply.
Renouncing a policy of boorish indifference
to everything that has been said since the days of Matilda,
I shall purchase an Etymological Dictionary of Modern English
that I may understand what is written
and like the ant and the spider
returning from time to time to headquarters,
shall answer the question
as to "why I like winter better than I like summer"
and acknowledge that it does not make me sick
to look modern playwrights and poets and novelists straight in
                                                        the face—
that I feel just the same;
and I shall write to the publisher of the magazine
which will "appear the first day of the month

and disappear before one has had time to buy it
unless one takes proper precaution,"
and make an effort to please—
since he who gives quickly gives twice
in nothing so much as in a letter.

NOVICES

anatomize their work
in the sense in which Will Honeycomb was jilted by a duchess,
the little assumptions of the scared ego confusing the issue
so that they do not know "whether it is the buyer or the seller
                                        who gives the money"—
an abstruse idea plain to none but the artist,
the only seller who buys, and holds on to the money.
Because one expresses oneself and entitles it wisdom, one is not a
                            fool. What an idea!
"Dracontine cockatrices, perfect and poisonous from the
                                        beginning,"
they present themselves as a contrast to sea-serpented regions
                        "unlit by the half-lights of more conscious art."
Acquiring at thirty what at sixty they will be trying to forget,
blind to the right word, deaf to satire
which like "the smell of the cypress strengthens the nerves of the
                                        brain,"
averse from the antique
with "that tinge of sadness about it which a reflective mind
                                    always feels,
it is so little and so much"—
they write the sort of thing that would in their judgment interest
                                    a lady;
curious to know if we do not adore each letter of the alphabet
                        that goes to make a word of it—
according to the Act of Congress, the sworn statement of the
                            treasurer and all the rest of it—
the counterpart to what we are:

stupid man; men are strong and no one pays any attention:
stupid woman; women have charm and how annoying they
                                                        can be.
Yes, "the authors are wonderful people, particularly those that
                                                  write the most,"
the masters of all languages, the supertadpoles of expression.
Accustomed to the recurring phosphorescence of antiquity,
the "much noble vagueness and indefinite jargon" of Plato,
the lucid movements of the royal yacht upon the learned scenery
                                                        of Egypt—
king, steward, and harper seated amidships while the jade and
                        the rock crystal course about in solution,
their suavity surmounts the surf—
the willowy wit, the transparent equation of Isaiah, Jeremiah,
                                                Ezekiel, Daniel.
Bored by "the detailless perspective of the sea," reiterative and
                                                        naïve,
and its chaos of rocks—the stuffy remarks of the Hebrews—
the good and alive young men demonstrate the assertion
that it is not necessary to be associated with that which has
                                                        bored one;
they have never made a statement which they found so easy to
                                                        prove—
"split like a glass against a wall"
in this "precipitate of dazzling impressions,
the spontaneous unforced passion of the Hebrew language—
an abyss of verbs full of reverberations and tempestuous
                                                        energy,"
in which action perpetuates action and angle is at variance with
                                                        angle
till submerged by the general action;
obscured by "fathomless suggestions of color,"
by incessantly panting lines of green, white with concussion,
in this drama of water against rocks—this "ocean of hurrying
                                                consonants"

with its "great livid stains like long slabs of green marble,"
its "flashing lances of perpendicular lightning and "molten fires
                                                    swallowed up,"
"with foam on its barriers,"
"crashing itself out in one long hiss of spray."

MARRIAGE

This institution,
perhaps one should say enterprise
out of respect for which
one says one need not change one's mind
about a thing one has believed in,
requiring public promises
of one's intention
to fulfill a private obligation:
I wonder what Adam and Eve
think of it by this time,
this firegilt steel
alive with goldenness;
how bright it shows—
"of circular traditions and impostures,
committing many spoils,"
requiring all one's criminal ingenuity
to avoid!
Psychology which explains everything
explains nothing
and we are still in doubt.
Eve: beautiful woman—
I have seen her
when she was so handsome
she gave me a start,
able to write simultaneously
in three languages—
English, German and French
and talk in the meantime;

equally positive in demanding a commotion
and in stipulating quiet:
"I should like to be alone";
to which the visitor replies,
"I should like to be alone;
why not be alone together?"
Below the incandescent stars
below the incandescent fruit,
the strange experience of beauty;
its existence is too much;
it tears one to pieces
and each fresh wave of consciousness
is poison.
"See her, see her in this common world,"
the central flaw
in that first crystal-fine experiment,
this amalgamation which can never be more
than an interesting impossibility,
describing it
as "that strange paradise
unlike flesh, gold, or stately buildings,
the choicest piece of my life:
the heart rising
in its estate of peace
as a boat rises
with the rising of the water";
constrained in speaking of the serpent—
that shed snakeskin in the history of politeness
not to be returned to again—
that invaluable accident
exonerating Adam.
And he has beauty also;
it's distressing—the O thou
to whom, from whom,
without whom nothing—Adam;

"something feline,
something colubrine"—how true!
a crouching mythological monster
in that Persian miniature of emerald mines,
raw silk—ivory white, snow white,
oyster white and six others—
that paddock full of leopards and giraffes—
long lemonyellow bodies
sown with trapezoids of blue.
Alive with words,
vibrating like a cymbal
touched before it has been struck,
he has prophesied correctly—
the industrious waterfall,
"the speedy stream
which violently bears all before it,
at one time silent as the air
and now as powerful as the wind."
"Treading chasms
on the uncertain footing of a spear,"
forgetting that there is in woman
a quality of mind
which as an instinctive manifestation
is unsafe,
he goes on speaking
in a formal, customary strain
of "past states, the present state,
seals, promises,
the evil one suffered,
the good one enjoys,
hell, heaven,
everything convenient
to promote one's joy."
There is in him a state of mind
by force of which,

perceiving what it was not
intended that he should,
"he experiences a solemn joy
in seeing that he has become an idol."
Plagued by the nightingale
in the new leaves,
with its silence—
not its silence but its silences,
he says of it:
"It clothes me with a shirt of fire."
"He dares not clap his hands
to make it go on
lest it should fly off;
if he does nothing, it will sleep;
if he cries out, it will not understand."
Unnerved by the nightingale
and dazzled by the apple,
impelled by "the illusion of a fire
effectual to extinguish fire,"
compared with which
the shining of the earth
is but deformity—a fire
"as high as deep as bright as broad
as long as life itself,"
he stumbles over marriage,
"a very trivial object indeed"
to have destroyed the attitude
in which he stood—
the ease of the philosopher
unfathered by a woman.
Unhelpful Hymen!
"a kind of overgrown cupid"
reduced to insignificance
by the mechanical advertising
parading as involuntary comment,

by that experiment of Adam's
with ways out but no way in—
the ritual of marriage,
augmenting all its lavishness;
its fiddle-head ferns,
lotus flowers, opuntias, white dromedaries,
its hippopotamus—
nose and mouth combined
in one magnificent hopper,
"the crested screamer—
that huge bird almost a lizard,"
its snake and the potent apple.
He tells us
that "for love
that will gaze an eagle blind,
that is like a Hercules
climbing the trees
in the garden of the Hesperides,
from forty-five to seventy
is the best age,"
commending it
as a fine art, as an experiment,
a duty or as merely recreation.
One must not call him ruffian
nor friction a calamity—
the fight to be affectionate:
"no truth can be fully known
until it has been tried
by the tooth of disputation."
The blue panther with black eyes,
the basalt panther with blue eyes,
entirely graceful—
one must give them the path—
the black obsidian Diana
who "darkeneth her countenance

as a bear doth,
causing her husband to sigh,"
the spiked hand
that has an affection for one
and proves it to the bone,
impatient to assure you
that impatience is the mark of independence
not of bondage.
"Married people often look that way"—
"seldom and cold, up and down,
mixed and malarial
with a good day and a bad."
"When do we feed?"
We occidentals are so unemotional,
we quarrel as we feed;
one's self quite lost,
the irony preserved
in "the Ahasuerus tête à tête banquet"
with its "good monster, lead the way,"
with little laughter
and munificence of humor
in that quixotic atmosphere of frankness
in which "Four o'clock does not exist
but at five o'clock
the ladies in their imperious humility
are ready to receive you";
in which experience attests
that men have power
and sometimes one is made to feel it.
He says, "What monarch would not blush
to have a wife
with hair like a shaving-brush?
The fact of woman
is not 'the sound of the flute
but every poison.'"

She says, " 'Men are monopolists
of stars, garters, buttons
and other shining baubles'—
unfit to be the guardians
of another person's happiness."
He says, "These mummies
must be handled carefully—
'the crumbs from a lion's meal,
a couple of shins and the bit of an ear';
turn to the letter M
and you will find
that 'a wife is a coffin,'
that severe object
with the pleasing geometry
stipulating space and not people,
refusing to be buried
and uniquely disappointing,
revengefully wrought in the attitude
of an adoring child
to a distinguished parent."
She says, "This butterfly,
this waterfly, this nomad
that has 'proposed
to settle on my hand for life.'—
What can one do with it?
There must have been more time
in Shakespeare's day
to sit and watch a play.
You know so many artists who are fools."
He says, "You know so many fools
who are not artists."
The fact forgot
that "some have merely rights
while some have obligations,"
he loves himself so much,

he can permit himself
no rival in that love.
She loves herself so much,
she cannot see herself enough—
a statuette of ivory on ivory,
the logical last touch
to an expansive splendor
earned as wages for work done:
one is not rich but poor
when one can always seem so right.
What can one do for them—
these savages
condemned to disaffect
all those who are not visionaries
alert to undertake the silly task
of making people noble?
This model of petrine fidelity
who "leaves her peaceful husband
only because she has seen enough of him"—
that orator reminding you,
"I am yours to command."
"Everything to do with love is mystery;
it is more than a day's work
to investigate this science."
One sees that it is rare—
that striking grasp of opposites
opposed each to the other, not to unity,
which in cycloid inclusiveness
has dwarfed the demonstration
of Columbus with the egg—
a triumph of simplicity—
that charitive Euroclydon
of frightening disinterestedness
which the world hates,
admitting:

"I am such a cow,
if I had a sorrow,
I should feel it a long time;
I am not one of those
who have a great sorrow
in the morning
and a great joy at noon";

which says: "I have encountered it
among those unpretentious
protégés of wisdom,
where seeming to parade
as the debater and the Roman,
the statesmanship
of an archaic Daniel Webster
persists to their simplicity of temper
as the essence of the matter:

  'Liberty and union
  now and forever';

the book on the writing-table;
the hand in the breast-pocket."

SILENCE

My father used to say,
"Superior people never make long visits,
have to be shown Longfellow's grave
nor the glass flowers at Harvard.
Self reliant like the cat—
that takes its prey to privacy,
the mouse's limp tail hanging like a shoelace from its mouth—
they sometimes enjoy solitude,
and can be robbed of speech
by speech which has delighted them.
The deepest feeling always shows itself in silence;
not in silence, but restraint."
Nor was he insincere in saying, "Make my house your inn."
Inns are not residences.

AN OCTOPUS

of ice. Deceptively reserved and flat,
it lies "in grandeur and in mass"
beneath a sea of shifting snow dunes;
dots of cyclamen red and maroon on its clearly defined
                                        pseudopodia
made of glass that will bend—a much needed invention—
comprising twenty-eight ice fields from fifty to five hundred feet
                                        thick,
of unimagined delicacy.
"Picking periwinkles from the cracks"
or killing prey with the concentric crushing rigor of the python,
it hovers forward "spider fashion
on its arms" misleadingly like lace;
its "ghostly pallor changing
to the green metallic tinge of an anemone starred pool."
The firtrees in "the magnitude of their root systems,"
rise aloof from these maneuvers "creepy to behold,"
austere specimens of our American royal families,
"each like the shadow of the one beside it.
The rock seems frail compared with their dark energy of life,"
its vermillion and onyx and manganese blue interior
                                        expensiveness
left at the mercy of the weather;
"stained transversely by iron where the water drips down,"
recognized by its plants and its animals.
Completing a circle,
you have been deceived into thinking that you have progressed,
under the polite needles of the larches

"hung to filter not to intercept the sunlight"—
met by tightly wattled spruce twigs
"conformed to an edge like clipped cypress
as if no branch could penetrate the cold beyond its company";
and dumps of gold and silver ore enclosing The Goat's Mirror—
that lady-fingerlike depression in the shape of the left human foot,
which prejudices you in favor of itself
before you have had time to see the others;
its indigo, pea-green, blue-green, and turquoise,
from a hundred to two hundred feet deep,
"merging in irregular patches in the middle lake
where like gusts of a storm
obliterating the shadows of the firtrees, the wind makes lanes of
                                                                    ripples."
What spot could have merits of equal importance
for bears, elk, deer, wolves, goats, and ducks?
Preempted by their ancestors,
this is the property of the exacting porcupine,
and of the rat "slipping along to its burrow in the swamp
or pausing on high ground to smell the heather";
of "thoughtful beavers
making drains which seem the work of careful men with shovels,"
and of the bears inspecting unexpectedly
ant hills and berry bushes.
Composed of calcium gems and alabaster pillars,
topaz, tourmaline crystals and amethyst quartz,
their den is somewhere else, concealed in the confusion
of "blue forests thrown together with marble and jasper and agate
as if whole quarries had been dynamited."
And farther up, in stag-at-bay position
as a scintillating fragment of these terrible stalagmites,
stands the goat,
its eye fixed on the waterfall which never seems to fall—
an endless skein swayed by the wind,
immune to force of gravity in the perspective of the peaks.

A special antelope
acclimated to "grottoes from which issue penetrating draughts
which make you wonder why you came,"
it stands its ground
on cliffs the color of the clouds, of petrified white vapor—
black feet, eyes, nose, and horns engraved on dazzling ice-fields,
the ermine body on the crystal peak;
the sun kindling its shoulders to maximum heat like acetylene,
                              dyeing them white—
upon this antique pedestal—
"a mountain with those graceful lines which prove it a volcano,"
its top a complete cone like Fujiyama's
till an explosion blew it off.
Maintaining many minds, distinguished by a beauty
of which "the visitor dare never fully speak at home
for fear of being stoned as an imposter,"
Big Snow Mountain is the home of a diversity of creatures:
those who "have lived in hotels
but who now live in camps—who prefer to";
the mountain guide evolving from the trapper,
"in two pairs of trousers, the outer one older,
wearing slowly away from the feet to the knees";
"the nine-striped chipmunk
running with unmammallike agility along a log";
the water ouzel
with "its passion for rapids and high pressured falls,"
building under the arch of some tiny Niagara;
the white-tailed ptarmigan "in winter solid white,
feeding on heather bells and alpine buckwheat";
and the eleven eagles of the west,
"fond of the spring fragrance and the winter colors,"
used to the unegoistic action of the glaciers
and "several hours of frost every midsummer night."
"They make a nice appearance, don't they,"
happy seeing nothing?

Perched on treacherous lava and pumice—
those unadjusted chimney-pots and cleavers
which stipulate "the names and addresses of persons to notify
in case of disaster—"
they hear the roar of ice and supervise the water
winding slowly through the cliffs,
the road "climbing like the thread
which forms the groove around a snail-shell,
doubling back and forth until where snow begins, it ends."
No "deliberate wide-eyed wistfulness" is here
among the boulders sunk in ripples and white water
where "when you hear the best wild music of the mountains
it is sure to be a marmot,"
the victim on some slight observatory,
of "a struggle between curiosity and caution,"
inquiring what has scared it:
a stone from the moraine descending in leaps,
another marmot, or the spotted ponies with "glass eyes,"
brought up on frosty grass and flowers
and rapid draughts of ice water.
Instructed none knows how, to climb the mountain,
by "business men who as totemic scenery of Canada,
require for recreation,
three hundred and sixty-five holidays in the year,
these conspicuously spotted little horses are peculiar;
hard to discern among the birch trees, ferns, and lily pads,
avalanche lilies, Indian paintbrushes,
bears' ears and kittentails,
and miniature cavalcades of chlorophylless fungi
magnified in profile on the mossbeds like moonstones in the water;
the cavalcade of calico competing
with the original American "menagerie of styles"
among the white flowers of the rhododendron surmounting rigid
                                                              leaves

upon which moisture works its alchemy,

transmuting verdure into onyx.
Larkspur, blue pincushions, blue peas, and lupin;
white flowers with white, and red with red;
the blue ones "growing close together
so that patches of them look like blue water in the distance":
this arrangement of colors
as in Persian designs of hard stones with enamel,
forms a pleasing equation—
a diamond outside and inside, a white dot;
on the outside, a ruby; inside, a red dot;
black spots balanced with black
in the woodlands where fires have run over the ground—
separated by aspens, cat's paws, and woolly sunflowers,
fireweed, asters, and Goliath thistles
"flowering at all altitudes as multiplicitous as barley,"
like pink sapphires in the pavement of the glistening plateau.
Inimical to "bristling, puny, swearing men
equipped with saws and axes,"
this treacherous glass mountain
admires gentians, ladyslippers, harebells, mountain dryads,
and "Calypso, the goat flower—
that greenish orchid fond of snow"—
anomalously nourished upon shelving glacial ledges
where climbers have not gone or have gone timidly,
"the one resting his nerves while the other advanced,"
on this volcano with the bluejay, her principal companion.
"Hopping stiffly on sharp feet" like miniature icehacks—
"secretive, with a look of wisdom and distinction, but a villain,
fond of human society or the crumbs that go with it,"
he knows no Greek,
"that pride producing language,"
in which "rashness is rendered innocuous, and error exposed
by the collision of knowledge with knowledge."
"Like happy souls in Hell," enjoying mental difficulties,
the grasshoppers of Greece

amused themselves with delicate behavior
because it was "so noble and so fair";
not practiced in adapting their intelligence
to eagle traps and snowshoes,
to alpenstocks and other toys contrived by those
"alive to the advantage of invigorating pleasures."
Bows, arrows, oars, and paddles for which trees provide the wood,
in new countries are more eloquent than elsewhere—
augmenting evidence for the assertion
that essentially humane,
"the forest affords wood for dwellings and by its beauty stimulates
the moral vigor of its citizens."
The Greeks liked smoothness, distrusting what was back
of what could not be clearly seen,
resolving with benevolent conclusiveness,
"complexities which still will be complexities
as long as the world lasts";
ascribing what we clumsily call happiness,
to "an accident or a quality,
a spiritual substance or the soul itself,
an act, a disposition, or a habit,
or a habit infused to which the soul has been persuaded,
or something distinct from a habit, a power—"
such power as Adam had and we are still devoid of.
"Emotionally sensitive, their hearts were hard";
their wisdom was remote
from that of these odd oracles of cool official sarcasm,
upon this game preserve
where "guns, nets, seines, traps and explosives,
hired vehicles, gambling and intoxicants are prohibited,
disobedient persons being summarily removed
and not allowed to return without permission in writing."
It is self evident
that it is frightful to have everything afraid of one;
that one must do as one is told

and eat "rice, prunes, dates, raisins, hardtack, and tomatoes"
if one would "conquer the main peak" of Mount Tacoma
this fossil flower concise without a shiver,
intact when it is cut,
damned for its sacrosanct remoteness—
like Henry James "damned by the public for decorum";
not decorum, but restraint;
it was the love of doing hard things
that rebuffed and wore them out—a public out of sympathy with
neatness.
Neatness of finish! Neatness of finish!
Relentless accuracy is the nature of this octopus
with its capacity for fact.
"Creeping slowly as with meditated stealth,
its arms seeming to approach from all directions,"
it receives one under winds that "tear the snow to bits
and hurl it like a sandblast,
shearing off twigs and loose bark from the trees."
Is tree the word for these strange things
"flat on the ground like vines";
some "bent in a half circle with branches on one side
suggesting dustbrushes, not trees;
some finding strength in union, forming little stunted groves,
their flattened mats of branches shrunk in trying to escape"
from the hard mountain "planed by ice and polished by the
wind"—
the white volcano with no weather side;
the lightning flashing at its base,
rain falling in the valleys, and snow falling on the peak—
the glassy octopus symmetrically pointed,
its claw cut by the avalanche
"with a sound like the crack of a rifle,
in a curtain of powdered snow launched like a waterfall."

SEA UNICORNS AND LAND UNICORNS

with their respective lions—
"mighty monoceroses with immeasured tayles"—
these are those very animals
described by the cartographers of 1539,
defiantly revolving
in such a way that the hard steel
in the long keel of white exhibited in tumbling,
disperses giant weeds
and those sea snakes whose forms looped in the foam, "disquiet
shippers."
Not ignorant of how a voyager obtained the horn of a sea unicorn
to give Queen Elizabeth
who thought it worth a hundred thousand pounds,
they persevere in swimming where they like,
finding the place where lions live in herds,
strewn on the beach like stones with lesser stones—
and bears are white;
discovering Antarctica, its penguin kings and icy spires,
and Sir John Hawkins' Florida
"abounding in land unicorns and lions,
since where the one is,
its arch enemy cannot be missing."
Thus personalities by nature much opposed,
can be combined in such a way
that when they do agree, their unanimity is great,
"in politics, in trade, law, sport, religion,
china collecting, tennis, and church going."
You have remarked this fourfold combination of strange animals,

upon embroideries,
enwrought with "polished garlands" of agreeing indifference—
thorns, "myrtle rods, and shafts of bay,"
"cobwebs, and knotts, and mulberries"
of lapislazuli and pomegranate and malachite—
Britannia's sea unicorn with its rebellious child
now ostentatiously indigenous of the new English coast
and its land lion oddly tolerant of those pacific counterparts to it,
the water lions of the west.
This is a strange fraternity—these sea lions and land lions,
land unicorns and sea unicorns:
the lion civilly rampant,
tame and concessive like the long-tailed bear of Ecuador—
the lion standing up against this screen of woven air
which is the forest:
the unicorn also, on its hind legs in reciprocity.
A puzzle to the hunters, is this haughtiest of beasts,
to be distinguished from those born without a horn,
in use like Saint Jerome's tame lion, as domestics,
rebelling proudly at the dogs
which are dismayed by the chain lightning
playing at them from its horn—
the dogs persistent in pursuit of it as if it could be caught,
"deriving agreeable terror" from its "moonbeam throat"
on fire like its white coat and unconsumed as if of salamander's
skin.

So wary as to disappear for centuries and reappear,
yet never to be caught,
the unicorn has been preserved
by an unmatched device
wrought like the work of expert blacksmiths,
with which nothing can compare—
this animal of that one horn
throwing itself upon which head foremost from a cliff,
it walks away unharmed,

proficient in this feat, which like Herodotus,
I have not seen except in pictures.
Thus this strange animal with its miraculous elusiveness,
has come to be unique,
"impossible to take alive,"
tamed only by a lady inoffensive like itself—
as curiously wild and gentle;
"as straight and slender as the crest,
or antlet of the one-beam'd beast."
Upon the printed page,
also by word of mouth,
we have a record of it all
and how, unfearful of deceit,
etched like an equine monster on an old celestial map,
beside a cloud or dress of Virgin-Mary blue,
improved "all over slightly with snakes of Venice gold,
and silver, and some O's,"
the unicorn "with pavon high," approaches eagerly;
until engrossed by what appears of this strange enemy,
upon the map, "upon her lap,"
its "mild wild head doth lie."

NOTES

INDEX

NOTES

TO A PRIZE BIRD, p. 7
Bernard Shaw

INJUDICIOUS GARDENING, p. 8
Letters of Robert Browning and Elizabeth Barrett (Harper), Vol. I, p. 513: "the yellow rose? 'Infidelity,' says the dictionary of flowers." Vol. II, p. 38: "I planted a full dozen more rose-trees, all white—to take away the yellow-rose reproach!"

TO A STRATEGIST, p. 10
Disraeli

TO A STEAM ROLLER, p. 15
"impersonal judgment": Lawrence Gilman

TO A SNAIL, p. 17
"compression is the first grace of style": Demetrius

"method of conclusions," "knowledge of principles": Duns Scotus

"THE BRICKS ARE FALLEN DOWN," p. 18
Isaiah 9:10

GEORGE MOORE, p. 19
Vale (Appleton, 1914), p. 82. "We certainly pigged it together, pigs no doubt, but aspiring pigs."

"NOTHING WILL CURE THE SICK LION," p. 20
Carlyle

TO THE PEACOCK OF FRANCE, p. 21
"taking charge," "anchorites": H. C. Chatfield-Taylor, *Molière: A Biography* (Chatto, 1907)

IN THIS AGE OF HARD TRYING, p. 22
"it is not the business of gods": Turgenev

THE MONKEY PUZZLER, p. 25
the Chile pine, *Araucaria imbricata*. Arauco—a territory in Araucanía which is in the southern part of Chile: *imbricatus*—crooked like a gutter, or roof tile; or laid one under another like tiles

"a certain proportion in the skeleton": Lafcadio Hearn, *Talks to Writers* (Dodd, Mead, 1920), p. 170

POETRY [1924 and 1925], pp. 26 and 28
Diary of Tolstoy (Dutton), p. 84: "Where the boundary between prose and poetry lies, I shall never be able to understand. The question is raised in manuals of style, yet the answer to it lies beyond me. Poetry is verse: prose is not verse. Or else poetry is everything with the exception of business documents and school books."

POETRY [1924 only], p. 26
"literalists of the imagination": Yeats, "William Blake and His Illustrations to *The Divine Comedy*," *Ideas of Good and Evil* (1903), p. 182. "The limitation of his view was from the very intensity of his vision; he was a too literal realist of imagination, as others are of nature; and because he believed that the figures seen by the mind's eye, when exalted by inspiration were 'eternal existences,' symbols of divine essences, he hated every grace of style that might obscure their lineaments."

THE PAST IS THE PRESENT, p. 29
"Hebrew poetry is prose": The Reverend Edwin H. Kellogg

PEDANTIC LITERALIST, p. 30
All excerpts, from Richard Baxter, *The Saints' Everlasting Rest* (Lippincott, 1909)

"HE WROTE THE HISTORY BOOK," p. 31
At the age of five or six, John Andrews, son of Dr. C. M. Andrews, replied when asked his name: "My name is John Andrews. My father wrote the history book."

TO BE LIKED BY YOU, p. 34
"Attack is more piquant than concord": Hardy

SOJOURN IN THE WHALE, p. 36
"water in motion is far from level": *Literary Digest*

MY APISH COUSINS, p. 37
An old gentleman during a game of chess: "It is difficult to recall the appearance of what one might call the minor acquaintances twenty years back."

IN THE DAYS OF PRISMATIC COLOR, p. 47
"Part of it was crawling": Nestor, *Greek Anthology* (Loeb Classical Library), Vol. III, p. 129

PETER, p. 49
A black-and-white cat owned by Miss Magdalen Hueber and Miss Maria Weniger

PICKING AND CHOOSING, p. 53
feeling: T. S. Eliot, "In Memory," *The Little Review* (August, 1918). "James's critical genius comes out most tellingly in his mastery over, his baffling escape from, Ideas; a mastery and an escape which are perhaps the last test of a superior intelligence. He had a mind so fine that no idea could violate it. . . . In England ideas run wild and pasture on the emotions; instead of thinking with our feelings (a very different thing) we corrupt our feelings with ideas; we produce the political, the emotional idea, evading sensation and thought."

"sad French greens": *The Compleat Angler*

"top of a *diligence*": preparatory school boy translating Caesar; recollected by Mr. E. H. Kellogg

"right good salvo of barks," "strong wrinkles": Xenophon, *Cynegeticus*

ENGLAND, p. 55
"chrysalis of the nocturnal butterfly": Erté

"I envy nobody": *The Compleat Angler*

WHEN I BUY PICTURES, p. 57
snipe legged hieroglyphic: Egyptian low relief in The Metropolitan Museum

"A silver fence was erected by Constantine to enclose the grave of Adam": *Literary Digest* (January 5, 1918); a descriptive paragraph with photograph

Michael taking Adam: *Adam and Eve Taken by Michael out of Eden*, wash drawing by Blake

"lit by piercing glances": A. R. Gordon, *The Poets of The Old Testament* (Hodder and Stoughton, 1912)

THE LABORS OF HERCULES, p. 62
the piano: someone writes of the smooth polished case of the piano offering temptation to one as a child, to draw on it with a pin

"charming tadpole notes": review in the *London Spectator*

"the Negro is not brutal": The Reverend J. W. Darr

NEW YORK, p. 64
fur trade: in 1921, New York succeeded St. Louis as the center of the wholesale fur trade

"as satin needlework": *The Literary Digest* (March 30, 1918) quotes *Forest and Stream* (March 1918)—an article by George Shiras, 3rd: "Only once in the long period that I have hunted or photographed these animals (white-tailed deer) in this region, have I seen an albino, and that one lingered for a year and a half about my camp, which is situated midway between Marquette and Grand Island. Signs were put up in the neighborhood reading: 'Do not shoot the white deer—it will bring you bad luck.' But tho the first part of the appeal stayed the hand of the sportsman, and the latter that of most pot-hunters, it was finally killed by an unsuperstitious homesteader, and the heretofore unsuccessful efforts to photograph it naturally came to an end.

"Some eight years ago word came that a fine albino buck had been frequently seen on Grand Island and that it came to a little pond on the easterly part of the island. Taking a camping outfit, a canoe, and my guide, several days and nights were spent watching the pond; . . . the white buck did not appear.

"The next year the quest was no more successful, and when I heard that on the opening of the season the buck had been killed by a lumberjack, it was satisfactory to know that the body has been shipped to a taxidermist in Detroit, preparatory to being added to the little museum of the island hotel.

"About the middle of June, 1916, a white fawn only a few days old was discovered in a thicket and brought to the hotel. Here, in the company of another fawn, it grew rapidly. During the earlier months this fawn had the usual row of white spots on the back and sides, and altho there was no difference between these and the body color, they were conspicuous in the same way that satin needlework in a single color may carry a varied pattern. . . . In June, 1917, one of these does bore an albino fawn, which lacked, however, the brocaded spots which characterized the previous one.

"It may be of interest to note that the original buck weighed 150 pounds and possessed a rather extraordinary set of antlers, spreading twenty-six inches, with terminal points much further apart than any I have ever seen. The velvet on the antlers . . . was snow-white, giving them a most statuesque appearance amid the green foliage of the forest. The eyes of the three native albinos are a very light gray-blue, while the doe has the usual red eyeballs; . . . and in the absence of accident or disease, there should soon be a permanent herd of these interesting animals."

picardel: an Elizabethan ruff

"if the fur is not finer": Isabella, Duchess of Gonzaga. Frank Alvah Parsons, *The Psychology of Dress* (Doubleday), p. 68. "I wish black cloth even if it cost ten ducats a yard. If it is only as good as that which I see other people wear, I had rather be without it."

"accessibility to experience": Henry James

PEOPLE'S SURROUNDINGS, p. 65
"natural promptness": Ward, *English Poets*. Webbe—"a witty gentleman and the very chief of our late rhymers. Gifts of wit and natural promptness appear in him abundantly."

1420 pages: advertisement, *New York Times* (June 13, 1921). "Paper—As Long as a Man, As Thin as a Hair. One of the Lindenmeyr Lines was selected by Funk & Wagnalls Company, publishers of *The Literary Digest*, and *The Standard Diction-ary*, for their twelve page pamphlet on India Paper. India Paper is so extremely thin that many grew fearful of the results when the unwieldy size, 45x65 inches, was mentioned. No mill ever made so large a sheet of India Paper; no printer ever attempted to handle it. But S. D. Warren Company produced the paper and Charles Francis Press printed it—printed it in two colors with perfect register. Warren's India is so thin that 1420 pages make only one inch."

Persian velvet: Exhibition of Persian objects, Bush Terminal Building, December, 1919, under the auspices of the Persian Throne. Descriptive label—piece of 16th century brocaded velvet: "The design consists of single rose bushes in pearl white and pale black outline posed on a field of light brown ivory so that the whole piece bears the likeness of the leopard's spots."

Waterford: Irish glass

"a good brake": advertisement

municipal bat roost: experiment in San Antonio, Texas, to combat mosquitoes

"instant beauty": advertisement

Bluebeard's tower: limestone tower at St. Thomas, Virgin Islands; purports to be the castle of the traditional Bluebeard

"chessmen carved out of moonstones": Anatole France

"as an escalator cuts the nerve of progress": The Reverend J. W. Darr

"a setting": "The Perfect Host," *Vogue* (August 1, 1921)

captains of armies: Raphael, *Horary Astrology*

SNAKES, MONGOOSES, p. 68
"the slight snake": George Adam Smith

plastic animal: Hegel, *Philosophy of History*. The Greek state was plastic, i.e., all of a piece

BOWLS, p. 70
"appear the first day": advertisement in French magazine

NOVICES, p. 72
"Is it the buyer or the seller who gives the money?": Anatole France, *Petit Pierre*. Pierre's inquiry upon first visiting a chocolate shop

"dracontine cockatrices": Southey, *The Young Dragon*

"lit by the half lights of more conscious art": A. R. Gordon, *The Poets of the Old Testament*

"the smell of the cypress": Landor, "Petrarca," *Imaginary Conversations*, Camelot Series (Walter Scott Publishing Company), p. 52. "The smell of box, although not sweet, is more agreeable to me than many that are. . . . The cypress too seems to strengthen the nerves of the brain."

"that tinge of sadness": Arthur Hadyn, *Illustrated London News* (February 26, 1921). "The Chinese objects of art and porcelain dispersed by Messrs. Puttick and Simpson on the 18th, had that tinge of sadness which a reflective mind always feels; it is so little and so much."

"the authors are wonderful people": Leigh Hunt

"much noble vagueness": James Harvey Robinson, *The Mind in the Making*

"split like a glass against a wall": "Freaks of Fortune," *The Decameron*, introduction by Morley (Cassell, 1908)

"precipitate of dazzling impressions": A. R. Gordon, *The Poets of the Old Testament*

"fathomless suggestions of colour": P. T. Forsyth, *Christ on Parnassus* (Hodder and Stoughton)

"ocean of hurrying consonants": George Adam Smith, *Expositor's Bible*

"great livid stains": Faguet, *Gustave Flaubert* (Houghton, Mifflin)

"flashing lances," "molten fires": Leigh Hunt, *Autobiography*

"with foam on its barriers": George Adam Smith, *Expositor's Bible*

"crashing itself out": George Adam Smith, *Expositor's Bible*

MARRIAGE, p. 75
"of circular traditions": Francis Bacon

write simultaneously: "Multiple Consciousness or Reflex Action of Unaccustomed Range," *Scientific American* (January, 1922). "Miss A—— will write simultaneously in three languages, English, German, and French, talking in the meantime. [She] takes advantage of her abilities in everyday life, writing her letters simultaneously with both hands; namely, the first, third, and fifth words with her left and the second, fourth, and sixth with her right hand. While generally writing outward, she is able as well to write inward with both hands."

"See her, see her in this common world": "George Shock"

"unlike flesh, stones": Richard Baxter, *The Saints' Everlasting Rest* (Lippincott, 1909)

"something feline, something colubrine": Philip Littell, "Books and Things: Santayana's Poems," *New Republic* (March 21, 1923). "We were puzzled and we were fascinated, as if by something feline, by something colubrine."

"treading chasms": Hazlitt, essay on Burke's style

"past states": Baxter

"he experiences a solemn joy": Anatole France, "A Travers Champs," *Filles et Garçons* (Hachette). *"le petit Jean comprend qu'il est beau et cette idée le pénètre d'un respect profond de lui-même. . . . Il goûte une joie pieuse à se sentir devenu une idole."*

"it clothes me with a shirt of fire": Hagop Boghossian, "The Nightingale"

"he dares not clap his hands": Edward Thomas, *Feminine Influence on the Poets* (Martin Secker, 1910). "The Kingis Quair—To us the central experience is everything—the strong unhappy king, looking out of the prison window and seeing the golden-haired maiden in rich attire trimmed with pearls, rubies, emeralds and sapphires, a chaplet of red, white and blue feathers on her head, a heart-shaped ruby on a chain of fine gold hanging over her white throat, her dress looped up carelessly to walk in that fresh morning of nightingales in the new-leaved thickets—her little dog with his bells at her side."

"illusion of a fire": Baxter

"as high as deep": Baxter

"very trivial object": Godwin. "marriage is a law and the worst of all laws . . . a very trivial object indeed."

"a kind of overgrown cupid": Brewer, *Dictionary of Phrase and Fable*

"the crested screamer": remark in conversation, Glenway Wescott

"for love that will gaze an eagle blind": Anthony Trollope, *Barchester Towers*, Vol. II

"No truth can be fully known": Robert of Sorbonne

"darkeneth her countenance as a bear doth": "Women Bad and Good—An Essay," *Ecclesiasticus: The Modern Reader's Bible* (Macmillan)

"Married people often look that way": C. Bertram Hartmann

"seldom and cold": Baxter

"Ahasuerus tête à tête banquet": George Adam Smith, *Expositor's Bible*

"Good monster, lead the way": *The Tempest*

"Four o'clock does not exist": la Comtesse de Noailles, "le Thè," *Femina* (December, 1921). *"Dans leur impérieuse humilité elles jouent instinctivement leurs rôles sur le globe."*

"What monarch": "The Rape of the Lock," a satire in verse by Mary Frances Nearing with suggestions by M. Moore

"the sound of the flute": A. Mitram Rhibany, *The Syrian Christ.* Silence on the part of women—"to an Oriental, this is as poetry set to music" although "in the Orient as here, husbands have difficulty in enforcing their authority"; "it is a common saying that not all the angels in heaven could subdue a woman."

"men are monopolists": Miss M. Carey Thomas, President Emeritus of Bryn Mawr College, Founders address, Mount Holyoke College, 1921. "Men practically reserve for themselves stately funerals, splendid monuments, memorial statues, membership in academies, medals, titles, honorary degrees, stars, garters, ribbons, buttons and other shining baubles, so valueless in themselves and yet so infinitely desirable because they are symbols of recognition by their fellow craftsmen of difficult work well done."

"the crumbs from a lion's meal": Amos 3:12. Translation by George Adam Smith, *Expositor's Bible*

"a wife is a coffin": quoted by John Cournos from Ezra Pound

"settle on my hand": Charles Reade, *Christie Johnstone*

"some have rights": Morley, *Burke*, English Men of Letters Series

"leaves her peaceful husband": Simone A. Puget, "Change of Fashion," advertisement, *English Review* (June 1914). "Thus proceed pretty dolls when they leave their old home to renovate their frame, and dear others who may abandon their peaceful husband only because they have seen enough of him."

"Everything to do with love is mystery": F. C. Tilney, "Love and Folly": Book XII, No. 14, *The Original Fables of La Fontaine* (Dutton)

"I am such a cow": remark in conversation by Miss M. H. Tolman

"Liberty and Union": Daniel Webster

SILENCE, p. 84

My father used to say: a remark in conversation by Miss A. M. Homans, Professor Emeritus of Hygiene, Wellesley College. "My father used to say, 'superior people never make long visits, then people are not so glad when you've gone.' When I am visiting, I like to go about by myself. I never had to be shown Longfellow's grave nor the glass flowers at Harvard."

"*Make my house your inn*": Edmund Burke to a stranger with whom he had fallen into conversation in a bookshop. James Prior, *Life of Burke*. " 'Throw yourself into a coach,' said he. 'Come down and make my house your inn.' "

AN OCTOPUS, p. 85

glass that will bend: Sir William Bell of the British Institute of Patentees has made a list of inventions which he says the world needs. The list includes glass that will bend; a smooth road surface that will not be slippery in wet weather; a furnace that will conserve 95 per cent of its heat; a process to make flannel unshrinkable; a noiseless airplane; a motor engine of one pound weight per horse-power; methods to reduce friction; a process to extract phosphorus from vulcanized India rubber so that it can be boiled up and used again; practical ways of utilizing the tides

"*Picking periwinkles*": M. C. Carey, *London Graphic* (August 25, 1923)

"*spider fashion*": W. P. Pycraft, *Illustrated London News* (June 28, 1924)

"*ghostly pallor*": Francis Ward, *Illustrated London News* (August 11, 1923)

"*magnitude of their root systems*": John Muir

"*creepy to behold*": W. P. Pycraft

"*each like the shadow of the one beside it*": Ruskin

"*conformed to an edge*": W. D. Wilcox, *The Rockies of Canada* (Putnam, 1903)

"*thoughtful beavers*": Clifton Johnson, *What to See in America* (Macmillan)

"*blue stone forests*": Clifton Johnson, *What to See in America*

"*grottoes*": W. D. Wilcox, *The Rockies of Canada*

"two pairs of trousers": W. D. Wilcox. "My old packer, Bill Peyto. He usually wears two pairs of trousers, one over the other, the outer pair about six months older. Every once in a while, Peyto would give one or two nervous yanks at the fringe and tear off the longer pieces, so that his outer trousers disappeared day by day from below upwards."

"deliberate wide eyed wistfulness": Olivia Howard Dunbar, review of Alice Meynell's prose, *Post Literary Review* (June 16, 1923). "There is no trace here of deliberate wide eyed wistfulness."

marmot: W. P. Taylor, Assistant Biologist, Bureau of Biological Survey, U. S. Department of Agriculture. "The clear and penetrating whistle of the hoary marmot is perhaps the best wild music of the mountains."

"glass eyes": W. D. Wilcox. A colorless condition of the retina, characteristic of the Indian pony or cayuse

"business men": W. D. Wilcox. "A crowd of the business men of Banff, who usually take about 365 holidays every year, stands around to offer advice."

"menagerie of styles": W. M., "The Mystery of an Adjective and of Evening Clothes," *London Graphic* (June 21, 1924). "Even in the Parisian menagerie of styles there remains this common feature that evening dress is always evening dress in men's wear. With women there is no saying whether a frock is meant for tea, dinner, or for breakfast in bed."

"bristling, puny, swearing men": Clifton Johnson

"They make a nice appearance, don't they?": comment overheard at the circus

"Greek, that pride-producing language": Anthony Trollope, *An Autobiography* (Oxford University Press)

"rashness is rendered innocuous": Cardinal Newman, *Historical Sketches*

"Like happy souls in hell": Richard Baxter, *The Saints' Everlasting Rest*

"so noble and so fair": Cardinal Newman, *Historical Sketches*

"complexities . . . an accident": Richard Baxter

"The Greeks were emotionally sensitive": W. D. Hyde, *The Five Great Philosophies* (Macmillan)

"creeping slowly": Francis Ward

"tear the snow," "flat on the ground," "bent in a half circle": Clifton Johnson

"with a sound like the crack of a rifle": W. D. Wilcox

Quoted descriptions of scenery and of animals, of which the source is not given, have been taken from government pamphlets on our national parks

SEA UNICORNS AND LAND UNICORNS, p. 92
"mighty monoceroses": Spenser

"disquiet shippers": Violet A. Wilson—*Queen Elizabeth's Maids of Honour* (Lane)—quotes Olaus Magnus, *History of the Goths and Swedes*. "The sea serpent: he hath commonly hair hanging from his neck a cubit long, and sharp scales and is black, and he hath flameling shining eyes. This snake disquiets shippers and he puts up his head like a pillar, and catcheth away men."

a voyager: Violet A. Wilson, *Queen Elizabeth's Maids of Honour*. Thomas Cavendish: "He sailed up the Thames in splendour, the sails of his ship being cloth of gold and his seamen clad in rich silks. Many were the curiosities which the explorers brought home as presents for the ladies. The Queen naturally had first choice and to her fell the unicorn's horn valued at a hundred thousand pounds, which became one of the treasures of Windsor."

"abounding in land unicorns": Violet A. Wilson. "Hawkins affirmed the existence of land unicorns in the forests of Florida, and from their presence deducted abundance of lions because of the antipathy between the two animals, so that 'where the one is the other cannot be missing.'"

"in politics, in trade": Henry James, *English Hours*

"polished garlands," "myrtle rods": J. A. Symonds

"cobwebs, and knotts, and mulberries": Queen Elizabeth's dresses. Violet A. Wilson, *Queen Elizabeth's Maids of Honour*. "A forepart of white satten, embrodered all over with pansies, little roses, knotts, and a border of mulberries, pillars, and pomegranets, of Venice golde, sylver, and sylke of sondrye colours. One forepart of green satten embroidered all over with sylver, like beasts, fowles, and fishes." "A petticoat embroidered all over slightly with snakes of Venice gold and silver and some O's, with a faire border embroidered like seas, cloudes, and rainbowes."

the long tailed bear of Ecuador: In his *Adventures in Bolivia* (Lane, 1922), p. 193, C. H. Prodgers tells of a strange animal that he bought: "It was stuffed with long grass and cost me ten shillings, turning out eventually to be a bear with a tail. In his book on wild life, Rowland Ward says, 'Amongst the rarest animals is a bear with a tail; this animal is known to exist, is very rare, and only to be found in the forest of Ecuador,' and this was where the man who sold it to me said he got it."

"deriving agreeable terror": Leigh Hunt. "The lover of reading will derive agreeable terror from Sir Bertram and The Haunted Chamber."

"moonbeam throat": "Medieval"—anonymous poem in *Punch* (April 25, 1923)

an unmatched device: *Bulfinch's Mythology.* "Some described the horn as movable at the will of the animal, a kind of small sword in short, and which no hunter who was not exceedingly cunning in fence could have a chance. Others maintained that all the animal's strength lay in its horn, and that when hard pressed in pursuit it would show itself from the pinnacle of the highest rocks horn foremost, so as to pitch on it, and then quietly march off not a whit the worse for its fall."

Herodotus says of the phoenix: "I have not seen it myself except in a picture."

"impossible to take alive": Pliny

"as straight": Charles Cotton, "An Epitaph on M. H.

    As soft, and snowy, as that down
    Adorns the Blow-ball's frizzled crown;
    As straight and slender as the crest,
    Or antlet of the one-beam'd beast;"

"improved all over": see "cobwebs"

"with pavon high," "upon her lap": "Medieval"—anonymous poem in *Punch* (April 25, 1923)

INDEX